Glimpses

Glimpses

short stories, poetry, & essays

Vaughn F. Keller

Riverhaven Books
www.RiverhavenBooks.com

These stories are works of fiction. The characters, events, and locales are products of the author's imagination or are used fictitiously and any resemblance to actual persons, living or dead, events, or locales is purely coincidental. The poems? Well, they are poems. As for the essays, no offense is meant.

Copyright© 2012 by Vaughn Keller

All rights reserved.

Published in the United States by
Riverhaven Books,
www.RiverhavenBooks.com

ISBN: 978-1-937588-16-8

Printed in the United States of America
by Country Press, Lakeville, Massachusetts

Designed and Edited by
Stephanie Lynn Blackman
Whitman, MA

For my father

Herbert S. Keller

He read everything

Preface

I envy friends and family members who are skilled at making things, especially at Christmas. I imagine the production lines set up in their kitchens and workrooms turning out hundreds of cookies, crafts, and all sorts of clever presents. Oh, to be so talented! Christmas never poses a problem for them. Once they get the idea, a good chunk of their work is done. Then, if they can enlist other family members to contribute some labor, they are halfway to wrapping presents.

I am not blessed with these talents. No production lines. Not even a hint of a brilliant idea that Martha Stewart would approve of, or perhaps even applaud.

So what to do? Well, for better or for worse, I do write. Sometimes well; sometimes not so well; and often, too often perhaps, I can't tell the difference. I do it throughout the year, but still, pulling things together and wondering if there is enough that's of sufficient value to make a respectable little Christmas collection is always a question. You will have to judge that for yourself.

The stories are all new. There are new poems here as well, but I have resurrected some older ones and feel justified in including them because I have done some re-writing. The essays span the years.

These, then, are glimpses – quick takes, out of the corner of my eye.

Table of Contents

Hot Time in the City	1
LaGuardia September 11, 2006	7
Blue Hill Fair	10
Coffee Mate	12
The Hard "Truth"	13
Maggie's Niece	28
Maggie's Diner	30
Sarah at Chanukah, 1993	42
Creation, Compassion, and Commitment: Towards a Cosmology of Social Transformation	44
Getting Even	76
Daffodils	98
I Wish I Had My Camera With Me	99
The Truth is Enough	101
Hear Him Out	104
Why Liberal Religion Will Disappear	106
Heathrow	126
Thanksgiving at Little Rock	132
Sicko – Another Lover's Quarrel From Michael Moore	143
November	146
The Knee and the Boat	148
Center Harbor	159
Revolution and Evolution	160

Hot Time in the City

Ninety-five degrees of summer heat in New York City is skin crawly, can't breathe, let me out of here ugly. It is gray heat, not like the same heat in the suburbs where seeing green and feeling green under your feet, rather than concrete, somehow makes it less ugly.

The smells of the city become more intense, and on West Forty-Ninth Street, half a block down from Eleventh Avenue, the smell of the stables from horses and rarely cleaned buggies parked on the street weren't perfume to Nancy. The penetrating smell of horse manure elevated the degree of annoyance she felt at Basilio for parking the bus there after they dropped the "guests" off at Eighth Avenue and Forty-Sixth Street so they could go to their Saturday matinees. For many it would be the first Broadway shows they had ever seen.

She couldn't say much. When the guests weren't on board, he was in charge of the bus. It was his decision. She had been complaining about him to her boss for three trips now and had been told to stop whining. Guests liked him. He stuck to the timetable, didn't have any accidents, didn't drink, and showed up. That was big: showing up. The implication was clear. Tour guides were easier to find than reliable drivers.

Company policy prohibited keeping the engine running for more than fifteen minutes when you were parked. For three hours there would be no air conditioning in the bus, no windows to open. They needed shade. The luggage was at the hotel uptown so the compartments in the belly of the bus were empty. Basilio opened the compartment doors on both sides to catch any stirring of a breeze. There was no breeze. Basilio stretched out on his back in one of the compartments, legs dangling into the street. In her compartment, Nancy curled into a ball, uncurled, tucked her skirt between her legs to sop up sweat, and fantasized about her mother's lawn and the swing between the two oak trees in Rockport, just North of Boston.

Her son, his wife, and their two children would be there by now. Vacation time. She missed being with them, but she had to work. It was summer and the "Great Eastern Cities" tours were filled for July and August. She needed the work. Ten years ago she had gotten out of her marriage quickly, too quickly to think through getting older, retiring, and then old age. At sixty-eight she was a talking machine, talking from Boston to New York to Philadelphia to Washington, D.C. – the great Eastern Cities. She supposed they were, but right now she was tired of talking about them.

She was dozing and didn't notice the shirtless man crawl into her compartment with her. She smelled him first, then heard him before she opened her eyes and saw him – a long, dirty beard on a skinny face looking at her. He didn't say anything. They stared at one another as Nancy registered that a dirty, smelly, strange man without a shirt was in her compartment.

"Get out of here. Who are you? Leave. Basilio!" The last was a scream. She banged her fist on the wall that separated the two compartments. There was no answer. She scrambled out of the compartment and tripped over the man's shopping cart with his belongings. She fell on to the pavement and scraped her right knee banging it painfully into the concrete. "Basilio!" Another scream. No answer.

She got to her feet, her knee almost buckling under her and looked into the compartment where Basilio had been sleeping. He wasn't there. *Bastard must have gone for a walk and left me here alone*, she thought. The man in the luggage compartment still hadn't said anything.

She turned back to where he continued to stare at her. "Get out of here. Go! Now!"

He shifted a little and hunched back more towards the center of the compartment. "It's hot." His voice was hoarse and low.

"You can't stay here. We have to pick up people. You have to leave now," she reasoned with him. She heard, or felt, Basilio behind her.

"What the hell is going on?"

"He won't leave. He crawled in right next to me. Where were you?"

"I went to get some cold water. Here." He handed her a large bottle of water.

He turned to the man in the luggage compartment, "You. Get out of there before I drag you out."

The man started to move away from Basilio, towards the road side of the compartment, but made no move to get out.

"I said get out of there and I meant it, or I'll come in and drag your sorry ass the hell out of there."

"It's hot."

Basilio reached into the compartment, but the man was too far on the other side so Basilio climbed in and tried to grab a leg, but the man kicked back at him. Basilio pulled back to avoid the kicking.

"Okay. You've asked for it." Basilio crawled out and reached into the compartment where he had been sleeping and pulled out a pole with a hook on the end of it that he used to retrieve luggage.

He used it to start poking at the man, trying to force him out into the street. It worked. The man moved farther away towards the street to avoid the hook. He tried kicking it away as he moved. The hook caught onto the top of his left boot and he tried to shake it away. Basilio stopped pushing and started pulling.

"Got you sucker." Basilio laughed. It had turned into a game. Basilio pulled as hard as he could. The man slid towards him on the slick metal bottom of the empty compartment.

"Basilio stop it. You're going to hurt him."

"I've caught me a whale." Basilio pulled harder, backing up away from the bus as fast as he could. The man tried kicking the hook off but couldn't.

"Stop. Leave me…" It was too late. Basilio had pulled him out of the bus and the man hit the back of his head on the sharp curve where he landed. He stopped moving. Basilio dropped the pole.

Nancy saw it first. "He's bleeding." Basilio and Nancy both stared at the red circle forming around the head of the man. "Call 911," Nancy shouted. Tears started to form.

"No way. Get in the bus. We got to get out of here. Cops come we'll never get to our pick up." Basilio grabbed the pole and threw it into the compartment and closed the door.

"What are you doing?"

"We're out of here. Get the compartment doors. I'll open the bus."

Nancy stood still looking at him.

"Now," Basilio shouted. "Get moving. Move damn it."

Nancy stayed still.

"Damn it. Move." Basilio closed the second compartment and ran around to the other side of the bus. He closed one door, then another. Nancy didn't move. She stared at the pool of blood forming in the gutter.

Basilio opened the door to the bus with his key, climbed in, and started the diesel. He climbed back down and came over to Nancy. "We have to go now."

"I'm going to call 911."

"Wait 'til we're moving and tell them we saw this guy on the street. Now get in the bus. This isn't our fault. He climbed into our bus."

She followed him into the bus, wiping away the tears as she settled into her tour guide seat just above the door. Two blocks later she began to quiet and tried to focus on Rockport, her mother's green lawn, and the swing. By the time they reached the pick-up point she was there, gently swinging back and forth.

La Guardia September 11, 2006

Same airport. Same flight time. Same date, but five years later. Different terminal which I was grateful for. Five years ago we watched the monitor in the U.S. Air Terminal at LaGuardia. Smoke poured out of the North tower into a beautiful bright blue September sky. We walked to the windows and could see the two towers from the gate. A delay of all flights was announced. We continued to watch, wondering what had happened. The voice of the CNN announcer offered little more than that it was a two engine jet. How could this possibly happen?

We were still watching when the orange burst came out of the South Tower. The woman next to us screamed, "Oh my God. What's happening?" The tense had changed. It was now. A minute later there were two pillars of smoke defiling the September sky.

The order was given to evacuate the terminal. Buzz and I grabbed our roll aboards and computer bags and followed the others out onto the parking lot along Grand Central Parkway. We had been dropped off that morning by one of Bayer's limousines, usually a welcome convenience. Now we were stranded. A fellow passenger had a tiny portable radio. A small group of us gathered around him. The order had been given to close the bridges and tunnels in and out of the city so emergency vehicles could get through. All flights were grounded.

Then came the news of the Pentagon. "We're under attack." The word spread through the parking lot and the sounds of panic began to spread. Cell phones were everywhere. People walked away from the terminal like it had a contagious disease. Buzz decided to walk across the bridge to the hotels on the other side of the parkway to see if he could get us a room. He returned within fifteen minutes. All rooms along the strip were filled and one of the hotels was now tripling its rates.

I called Mary Ann to see if she could come in from Huntington where she was working that year to pick us up. No. All roads heading into the City were closed so emergency vehicles could get in from all over Long Island.

A plane was down in Pennsylvania. A Budget bus came around the corner. I flagged it down. Did they have any cars? No, but she thought there might be a pick up truck. I said I'd take it.

Cell phones were now barely working. The traffic was overwhelming the systems. A call came in from Buzz's office. Could he get back as soon as possible? Bayer was moving into public crisis mode. My traveling companion that day, Buzz Goodstein, was the Vice President of Scientific Relations at Bayer. He had been involved in the planning for the massive distribution of Cipro during and after Desert Storm. He was needed. We were under attack.

The only way to get him there was on a ferry or private boat. I called Mary Ann. A few minutes later she called back. There was no way to get a vehicle on for the next two days but he could get on as a walk on. We made arrangements for him to be picked up in Bridgeport. We got the pick up at Budget and headed for Port Jefferson.

Because of the ferry schedule, we had time to stop for lunch. We ate on the deck of a restaurant overlooking the harbor. A sense of unreality prevailed. The day was beautiful; the food was excellent; the view was lovely; the television set in the bar told of the horrors that were developing at the other end of Long Island Sound where we had just left.

I saw Buzz off and returned to Huntington. Mary Ann was already there. Schools had been let out. The television became our link to the world, a world that had changed.

This morning Mary Ann called just before my departure time to make sure everything was okay. LaGuardia was different, somehow quieter.

The TSA did not inspect our carry on luggage as we boarded this morning. I wish they had.

Blue Hill Fair
for Mary Ann

Too young, you learned to mend your own wounds,
    to cut away what was damaged,
    to stitch together
    the fragile membranes of duties and needs
    into a triumph worthy of a prize
    in the life craft division
    of any country fair in New England.

"Did you hear? Your friend's mom
    got the blue ribbon for life craft
    at the Blue Hill Fair."

The pain still comes when some self-involved soul
    doesn't look to see your back is bent
    and the scar tissue is stretched
    at the places where your nerves were cut.

So many of your roles respond to the "I need" in others.

Or, when the weather turns
    and a cold front moves in bringing change–
    thunder storms along the leading edge.

At times you stand your own tornado watch,
    anticipating the worse,
    fierce and protective.

Wasn't the weather lovely at the Blue Hill Fair this year?
We could smell the beginning of Fall
    as we watched the woman combing wool
    telling us of shedding rain and staying warm.

And every time you touched me I was grateful
    you chose not to amputate your heart
    as you wove together
    the triumph that's your life.

Driving home you read to me, we talked,
    and noted that the trees were changing color
    here in Maine, East of our homes,
    wonderfully away, but close enough for now.

Coffee Mate

I never vary how, day in and day out,
I make the coffee for my mate: honest.
Carefully, just the way the directions
On the insert instruct me to,
 I use the measure that came
Included with the pot.
Carefully I grind counting the seconds
Out loud to assure the beans will be coarse.
Yes,carefully, I pour the near, but not boiling, water
Into a measuring cup first to confirm
Only twelve ounces will be used.
My watch tells me my timer is accurate
As I stand with one hand poised ready
To push the plunger down at the timer's first beep
Coming at precisely two hundred and forty seconds.
In my heart I know, or at least I believe,
The staff of Starbuck's of Seattle would applaud.

And day in and day out for decades now
She tells me it is too weak or too strong
But maybe it is just for that day.
Still, I would think the law of averages,
The basic foundations of probability theory,
Would yield more than an occasional "perfect"
From this woman coming, still bed warm,
To meet the day, day in and day out.

The Hard "Truth"

In January of 1973 the staff at the national office of the Planned Parenthood Federation of America was called into the conference room for a momentous announcement. Harriet Pilpel had just called to report that the Supreme Court had issued a favorable decision in Roe v. Wade. Almost forty years later the debate continues, and it is anything but subdued. The simple frame: is abortion murder or an essential health service?

It is a unique debate. Experience and legal acceptance has not diminished the heat that it generates. Unlike racial inter-marriage, integrated schools, Title IX for women athletics, and other social changes, the citizens of the United States remain divided. In fact acceptance of abortion has diminished rather than grown. The issue polarizes and perplexes.

It is within this context that when I saw the cover of the Winter 2009 issue of UU World, I was intrigued. The cover announced an article by the Reverend Scotty McLennan that promised to defend abortion from a liberal Christian perspective. I quickly turned to the article and read it closely – several times. I found the article to be disappointing. Rather than a defense, what I found was a contradiction.

McLennan states his belief about the beginning of human life at two points in the article:

> *My personal religious understanding is that human life or personhood begins at birth, but I also think there are important protections that should be applied to potential human life at certain stages of fetal development.*

And later…

> *I'm also personally compelled by the notion that it's the breath of life that makes us full human beings. I'll never forget the sight of each of my children emerging into the world blue and lifeless, being struck on the back by the doctor, taking their first breath, and becoming ruddy-colored as they began crying their way into life. Now they were tiny people. Now they had joined the human race, not before.*

But he also states:

> *By the third trimester, though, the potential life has become viable; since the fetus could now live outside the womb, the state has a right to protect that potential life by prohibiting abortion except to preserve the life or health of the mother.*

In between these statements there is a recitation of the history of Jewish and Catholic teachings on abortion. This is not a "Christian Defense." There is history and the author's opinion. The "could live outside the womb" and "potential life" descriptions of the same phenomenon seem to contradict the notion that "life begins at birth." McLennan does not answer "why" the State should protect potential life and at no point explicates how Christian teaching informs the discussion.

I have become used to this. I believe that abortion is a much tougher issue than supporters of Choice have acknowledged. The recent debate around the Health Care Reform legislation highlighted the polarities that exist. I believe there is more rhetorical heat than logical thinking on both sides of the issue. As with many difficult issues the core dilemma is comprehensive and includes legal, ethical, and moral ramifications at multiple levels from the individual and the familial to the social. I do agree with McLennan that the question that draws the heat is: At what point and under what conditions does the State (you and me) have the right and the obligation to protect the fetus. Or, put another way, at one point and under what conditions does a woman lose her right to decide whether or not to carry the fetus to term or to abort?

The only condition that seems to gather close to universal support for abortion occurs rarely. Surveys indicate that most people support abortion if it is necessary to preserve the life and health of the mother. Logically, this is an unintended consequence argument. The intention is the preservation of the life and health of the mother; the unintended consequence is the death of the fetus through abortion.

The conditions that receive less support, but still majority support according to the surveys, are rape and incest. Here intention again comes into play. The premise is that the woman was a victim deprived of freedom and had no intention to engage in sex and certainly not to become pregnant through sex with the perpetrator. However, support for abortion in this situation does diminish according to the surveys because the intent of the abortion is focused on termination of the pregnancy. There is no assumption that the life or health of the mother is in jeopardy, at least physical health. Pro-life adherents struggle with this condition. The Catholic Church does not:

> *An unborn child is an innocent human, regardless of the circumstances of his conception. Though tragic, the crimes of rape or incest are only exacerbated, and the woman's torments are only intensified, by the additional sin of abortion. Since...the unborn is human, regardless of the "caliber" of his pre-born life, no alleged deficiency in his "quality" of life can justify the taking of that life.*
>
> *The same applies to the so-called "either/or" dilemma: The mother's life is supposedly in danger, and there is a chance she might die; to ensure her safety, it is said, it is necessary to kill the child. Yet one is never justified in doing evil that good may come of it (Rom. 3:8). What is at issue here is homicidal intent.*
>
> *[Some people allow] for abortions when the mother's "health" is in jeopardy. But what health? Physical*

only, when there is a likelihood of her death? Physical only, when there is no real likelihood of her death? Emotional? Besides, what is the definition of "jeopardy"? All mothers know that pregnancy inevitably brings "health" problems, if nothing more than nausea, varicose veins, and additional weight. The "mother's health" loophole is the greatest entree to abortion. [Catholic Answers]

The condition, though, that currently splits the citizens of the United States is when the intention to abort is voluntary. Support for abortion under this condition has steadily decreased.

Polls conducted in 2009 have found fewer Americans expressing support for abortion than in previous years. In Pew Research Center polls in 2007 and 2008, supporters of legal abortion clearly outnumbered opponents; now Americans are evenly divided on the question, and there have been modest increases in the numbers who favor reducing abortions or making them harder to obtain. Less support for abortion is evident among most demographic and political groups. [Pew Foundation]

I believe that one reason for this slippage is that an adequate argument for Choice has yet to be made. Although many arguments are proposed in support of Choice, I believe each of these arguments has flaws.

Before these arguments can be dissected, however, the word "life" must be considered. Life began sometime after the Big Bang and has continued. We don't know exactly when it began, but the archaeological record is clear that it was a very long time ago – billions of years. Let's be clear then that this debate is not about about "life." Everyone is pro-life unless they are quite mentally ill. Following this thread, we also know that sperm are quite lively and, if they were not, none of us would be here. I don't think, however, that anyone other than Woody Allen and people struggling with fertility are concerned with the life of the sperm. So what are people concerned about?

It is when the word *unique* comes into play that the fight begins. Scientifically this is also not debatable. A unique life begins at the moment of conception. The Catholic Church has that correct. The zygote, the scientific term, has a unique DNA unless it develops into identical twins, in which case the DNA is shared. It is alive by any definition of life: it grows, changes, and it is an open system exchanging energy with its environment. It is not, however, an independent life because at this point in our scientific development it is totally dependent upon the womb in which it is nested. In Western cultures it won't become truly independent until early adolescence, and we are extending adolescence all the time. So the argument should never have been about when life begins; it is about when you and I, the State, claim: "We have a right to exert influence over the progression of this life and we are going to tell you when our influence begins and when it ends."

One thing is certain: we are not going to wait until adolescence. We are also struggling with the exertion of our influence at the other end of the life span. Issues like assisted suicide are as perplexing.

The Supreme Court decision in Roe V. Wade was not terribly helpful because it relied on two principles. The first was "Privacy." Essentially the Court said that the development of this life was a private matter between the woman and her doctor during the first trimester of the pregnancy. However, the Court was relying on the science of the time and that is where some of the "ouch" enters in. The Court also said you and I (the State) could start to exert our influence during the second and third trimesters. So, essentially, total privacy ends at the end of the first trimester and then it is up to us, the State, whether we want to exert any influence after that. As a consequence we have fifty States given permission by the Court to establish laws regulating the availability and conditions for abortion during the second and third trimesters. Put another way, a woman in one state will have options that a woman in another state will not.

It is within this context that pro-choice advocates have been put in the position of having to generate arguments in favor of choice. Since attacks have been made on the basic premises in the court's decision, pro-choice proponents have had to defend abortion regardless of time, method, or condition. What follows are some of the arguments along with a discussion of the weaknesses of the arguments.

- One argument is that the right to have an abortion is the "law of the land." Therefore, any legislation at any level of government that restricts abortion is illegal. However, a replacement of one Supreme Court justice could change the "Law of the Land." "The Law of the Land" is a changing, political phenomenon. The Gore-Bush election and the decision of the Supreme Court to stop counting ballots is simply one example of how political an institution the court is. The history of the court also includes supporting separate but equal schooling. The "legal" defense of abortion is found wanting at many levels. The reliance in Roe v. Wade on privacy and science is especially troubling.

- The second argument that is used is scientific. During the first trimester fetal development is not sufficient to sustain life outside the womb. During the second trimester things get stickier for many people at an emotional level because towards the end of the second trimester the characteristics of the fetus become more similar to those we usually identify as uniquely human. Pain sensation, heart beats, brain activity, and movement are also measurable in the second trimester. In the third trimester viability external to the womb becomes more likely. The difficulty with the scientific argument is that supporters of choice are relying on a moving target. Pre-mature infants are kept alive today at younger and younger stages of development. It is not inconceivable that, in the future, artificial means of sustaining life will extend deeper into the second and perhaps first trimester. In other words, the inter-dependence of the fetus with a particular woman changes as science changes.

• The third argument is similar to the second but with a twist. The argument goes: If the fetus cannot sustain itself without artificial support then the woman has the right to abort or not abort the fetus because the fetus is not viable on its own. There are two difficulties with this argument. The first is that viability is idiosyncratic and unpredictable. Genes, health of the mother, pre-natal care, developmental history of the fetus, and the birth environment all come together to influence viability. One could use an average or a range and say, "Usually viability external to the womb occurs at thirty weeks." But that again becomes a moving target because it shifts from population to population of women. One also begins to encounter health paradoxes like the Hispanic paradox in which life expectancy is longer for

Hispanics than it "should be" given diet and medical care.

- The fourth argument is the prohibition argument. The premise is: If you do not make abortion safe and legal some women will still choose to abort as they have throughout history. The argument states: you will be restricting their access to essential health services that increase the likelihood that they will survive and be healthy. The premise is that without legal abortions, mortality and morbidity from unsafe abortions will increase. Therefore, there should be no prohibitions placed on the procedure. And, where does the State derive the authority to prohibit what is essentially a medical procedure?

This argument ignores that the State, you and me, prohibit all sorts of things, from selling alcohol and tobacco to teens to the distribution of controlled substances. In all of these cases an argument can be made that the prohibition itself causes unintended problems and there is no question that it does. Teens get older friends to buy alcohol for them. People buy bad dope and die from overdoses. The right to prohibit, then, is not in question, and the idea that prohibitions have unintended side effects is also not in question. However, what do we know about the consequences of prohibiting abortion? We have to go back in history. However, solid mortality and morbidity epidemiologic data associated with illegal abortions is difficult to obtain for several reasons: the procedure was illegal, the historical record is incomplete, and the professional community was not inclined to find out. Where there is data, it is on mortality and not morbidity. One citation from the CDC indicates that in 1969, four years prior to Roe V. Wade, there were thirty-one deaths in the United States from illegal abortions. While no death is acceptable, estimates of mortality and morbidity are illusive. We know that carrying a pregnancy to term and experiencing childbirth is more dangerous than legal abortion. We simply do not have data about illegal abortions. Unfortunately some of the statistics that are cited in the rhetorical wars to support pro-choice cannot be verified.

- The fifth argument is proprietorship. This argument operates from the premise that as long as the fetus is within the woman's body, the woman has the right of self-determination. A side argument is that it is her pregnancy and she has the right to do what she wants with the pregnancy.

This argument runs into several difficulties. First, the State restricts bodily proprietorship in many dimensions. We do not let people commit suicide and will hospitalize them if we believe they are a danger to themselves. Second, we clearly restrict the proprietorship of parents over their children and enact child abuse laws. The question, then, is how far back into the pregnancy does the right of the State extend? The child abuse line of thinking regarding the rights and obligations of parents has been extended, in some situations, to obligations during pregnancy.

We now know the consequences of alcohol abuse and drug abuse during pregnancy. There are cases which have found their way to the courts in which the rights of pregnant women to complete physical integrity have been challenged: In Whitner v. South Carolina the South Carolina State Supreme Court sided with the State that the State has a right and an obligation to protect the fetus from the harmful actions of the mother. This extension of child abuse considerations to a pregnant woman poses a dilemma for Choice supporters. As an example, even though McLennand in the UU World article advocates "breathing on its own" as the boundary, he at the same time advocates for the State's interest in protecting the fetus during the later stage of pregnancy.

- The final argument, one that is very compelling, is the argument of gender equity. There is no question that women bear the burden of pregnancy, childbirth, and child rearing in unequal proportion to the men who they had sex with. Because the balance of burden is so unequal, the argument goes, women must have the right to determine the consequences of the pregnancy. Or, "If I have the burden, I get to choose." One cannot argue with the analysis of burden. It is an accurate assessment of reality for women. One difficulty with its use as an argument in favor of "choice," however, is that it doesn't address the other arguments, especially the scientific argument. For how long into the pregnancy does the inequity privilege choice? And, what is sacrosanct about that particular boundary?

If extended, the burden argument is also an argument in favor of infanticide. Historically, infanticide was, and currently is, a response to the experience of burden. So the question must be asked: at one point does a woman lose her rights? Does the burden argument accept infanticide? The second problem with the argument is that if the burden argument is extended to all areas of human existence, inequity of burden becomes a justification for unique privilege. That is, a person with an inequitable burden has rights that another person does not. We already do this in some areas. Though minor by comparison, handicapped parking places are an example where unequal burden has been given a privilege. However, one quickly runs out of examples.

- In an ironic twist, Liberation Theologians, primarily Catholic, use the unequal burden argument in support of advocacy for the unique rights of the poor and use the teachings of Jesus to support their contention.

Given all of the weaknesses of the arguments, I remain firmly pro-choice. However, I do believe that the cogent pro-choice argument has yet to be made.

The best pro-choice argument I can come up with is not terribly comforting, but it is better than nothing. I had an opportunity many years ago to attend a retreat with the late Joseph Fletcher, the founder of Situational Ethics. While many things about the retreat were memorable, I will never forget Fletcher's response to the challenge: "What do you do when you have examined all sides of an issue for all stakeholders and you are still up in the air?" His answer was a question, "How is love best served?" I think love is best served by assuring women choice. However, if I adopt a rigorous "situational" stance, I have to leave an opening for immoral or unethical abortions, abortions in which love is not served. Designer babies is a possible example. However, my imagination starts to go numb at this point.

The situational stance does not eliminate the mess that you and I, as the State, must wrestle with to set boundaries. I do think it is best if we acknowledge that the issue is messy.

My teacher Ed Lynch used to say: "The truth is enough." I think the pro-choice movement would be best served by being painstakingly truthful, especially in this time of political lies. I am concerned that some of the protestations about the

Health Care Reform bill are political rather than truthful. Were women really "Thrown under the bus" by Obama and Pelosi as some of my dearest friends claim? I think a good case can be made that most women will be better off, even with the "deal" reaffirming the Hyde amendment that prohibits the use of Federal funds for abortion except under certain conditions. Did Obama and Pelosi use a situational stance in deliberating their choices? We know these are two very pragmatic politicians. I don't know if they asked "How is love best served?" but I do think they made situational tradeoffs.

I think there is a "truth" about the pro-choice position and I think it is a hard truth: *The pro-life argument is more satisfying intellectually.* A unique life begins at conception and it is the obligation of the State to protect that life. However, while intellectually satisfying, the pro-life argument is not empathic to the human condition. I believe this ambiguity is one we have to live with. My hypothesis is that we would be better off, personally and politically, if we acknowledged it. However, I will continue to get excited when I see an advertisement for an article that purports to present an intellectually cogent defense of Choice, and I will read it carefully.

Maggie's Diner

In winter the steam on the windows cracks the frost and
Tiny rivers flow down the glass
As the men come in for morning coffee -
      hooded sweatshirts, down vests,
      and a familiarity
      with one another as common
      as the clothes they wear.

The cold is left outside as talk turns to politics and sports and
Always the teasing and the nicknames of years spent together
      having morning coffee
      that gets set in front of you
      the minute you sit down.
There is no need to order here
      and any change would bring concern.

Owner Maggie gets and gives teasing
      with the professionalism of a
      nightclub comic and everyone
      was really worried about her
      when she wasn't there one morning
      and her sister filled in
      because Maggie was in the hospital
      having her gall bladder out.

She offered to show her four tiny scars when she returned
>   but there were no takers
>   and the men expressed their relief
>   with a simple, "Glad you're back."

It had only been a week but the world was out of joint
>   and her sister didn't tease much.

So Maggie doubled up for lost time
>   and everyone laughed again.

Maggie's Niece

The young woman sat across from him on the other side of one of the "U" shaped counter in Maggie's Diner. Ben was aware of her and looked up from his menu once or twice to peek before Maggie came over for his order. She hurriedly recited today's lunch specials for Ben. When she moved out of the way, heading back to the kitchen with his order of still one more Cobb Salad, Ben looked again at the young woman sitting opposite him. She wasn't beautiful or pretty. Maybe cute. No make-up, simple studs for earrings, no rings, short hair pulled straight back into a bun. She was wearing United States Army desert camo. She was staring straight ahead, through Ben, no focus. She sniffled a couple of times. Tear sniffles.

Maggie came back out with a bowl of something and placed it in front of her with some crackers. Ben could see her lips moving. Probably a soft, "Thank you." Maggie leaned across the counter and gave her a kiss on top of the head. More sniffles. She headed back to the kitchen. The girl closed her eyes and held her head. Her body tensed up as though she was ready to scream. After a minute or two she relaxed and began to eat.

A few minutes later Maggie brought Ben his salad. As she put it down she dropped her voice close to a whisper. "You still working at the law firm aren't you, Ben?"

"Yeah. Been close to a year now. Why, what's up?"

"That's what I thought. Look, I hate to impose, but would you be willing to talk to my niece. She's sitting at the counter right behind me and she's really upset." Ben had to lean forward to hear her.

Ben whispered back: "I thought she looked troubled. Problems?"

"That's just it. I don't know. She won't talk to anyone. I thought it might be a boyfriend or something, but she says no and she can't talk to me about it. I'm beginning to worry that she's in some kind of really serious trouble."

"Why do you think she'd talk to me? She doesn't know me from Adam."

"I don't know. I thought maybe a stranger might be easier. Someone closer to her age."

"I'm no therapist, Mag. I don't know."

"Yeah, I understand but you're easy to talk to. You always have been, ever since you were a kid and I'm really worried about her. There's nothing to lose by trying. She won't talk to anyone in the family."

"You sure I'm the person to do it? I mean I can give it a try, but if she won't talk to you… All I'm saying is don't expect too much."

Maggie put her hand on Ben's and gave it a gentle squeeze. "Thanks. You're a sweetheart."

"Okay if I tell her you sent me over? What's her name?"

"Nora. Named after my mother. She's my sister's oldest. I told her how I know you and that I was going to talk to you."

"What'd she say about that?"

"Nothing. Nothing at all. She doesn't talk. It's like she's numb"

"This sounds like it's way out of my league, Mag."

"Look, you're here. She's here. Why not? What's to lose?"

"Alright. I'll give it a try."

Ben swiveled around on his stool. It wobbled a little and creaked. He stood up and walked over to where Nora sat. One stripe, a private. She looked younger up close. Almost too young to be in uniform. Fresh out of high school young. He stood next to her and offered his hand.

"I'm Ben Kelly. Your aunt asked me if I would come over and say hello. I know this is weird because you don't know me, but I've known your aunt just about all my life and I know she's really worried about you. Okay if I sit down? She's hoping you might talk to me. Said you aren't talking to anyone else. I don't know why you would talk to me, but she asked me to try. I guess it's sort of a Hail Mary pass, you know, towards the end of the game. I suppose that makes me the football?" He was nervous. *Now I'm sounding weird*, he thought. *Talking too much.*

Nora looked up, saw Ben's outstretched hand, ignored it, and gave him a barely perceptible nod to sit down. He did.

They sat there side by side. Nora pushed her bowl of soup away and took a sip of her coffee once in awhile. Maggie brought Ben's salad and placed it in front of him. She gave very quick looks to both of them but didn't say anything and walked away to take care of another customer who had just come in.

There was a fan directly overhead, whirring slowly. Ben ate his salad. Maggie took the order from the new customer and brought it out ten minutes later. The new customer finished his lunch and left. Maggie collected all the ketchup bottles except for the one in front of Nora and Ben and got busy filling them.

Without any preliminaries Nora mumbled, "I don't know what to do."

Ben swiveled his stool so he could face her, "Do you want to tell me what's going on?"

Nora looked at him. "If I tell you, you going to tell my aunt?"

"Not if you don't want me to."

"You can't."

"Then I won't. I'm real good at secrets."

"I'm pregnant."

"And…"

"It's her son."

"Her son? You mean Maggie's son? Your cousin?"

"He's not really my cousin. He's her stepson."

"I take it this wasn't something you planned and there're some problems."

"Plenty."

"You okay talking about them?"

"No." The *no* carried finality with it. It was no to talking. No to Ben.

Ben waited to see if she would say anything more. When she didn't, he turned back to his salad, stabbed at the last couple of pieces of lettuce, ate them, and pushed the plate towards the center of the counter showing he was through. "You want to go for a walk. It's a nice day. We could just walk. Maybe talk, but only if you wanted to."

She gave him a puzzled look and stared at him before she said anything. She appeared to be sizing him up. Tall man. Dressed for a Saturday. Bit older than she was. Friend of Maggie's. "I guess. I don't want Maggie to think we might be talking. You go out first. Wait for me at the corner. Give me a couple of minutes and I'll catch up to you there."

"Okay."

Ben put seven dollars on the counter and shouted to Maggie, "Maggie. Got to go. See you." He stood up and walked out the door turning left, and then looking right. Which corner? You could see both. Didn't matter.

She was punctual. She looked left and then right, saw him and moved in his direction. They started walking. She started explaining right away. "He's married and he's got a new posting."

"Army?"

"It's the family business except for the diner, and that's Maggie's. She got it in her divorce from my uncle."

"Were you going to tell her about what's happened? That why you came here today?"

"Thought about it. Couldn't. He's her son. She raised him. He won't tell her that's for sure. I wanted to ask her what to do but I can't. He wants me to get an abortion. You know, keep it all secret.

I'm starting to throw up. Everyone's going to know."

"You're stationed nearby."

"Not too far away. New Jersey. Fort Dix."

"Have you talked to a chaplain?"

"No. I'm Catholic."

"I'm sure there's a priest."

"How am I going to talk to a priest about this? I know what he'll say. Have the baby. End of discussion."

Ben paused. "Got it. Tough place to be in. Talk to anybody?"

"Can't talk to my mother. Maggie's her sister. My dad would kill me. My brother would kill him."

"Kill him?"

"Yeah, if he knew, my brother would kill my cousin."

"Sounds like there's more."

"You can't say anything."

"Told you I wouldn't."

"He sort of raped me."

Ben stopped walking and looked at her as she walked away. She took three steps, stopped and walked back.

"Sort of?" Ben asked.

"You've got to understand. It's complicated."

"I'm trying but I'm not sure you should be talking to me about this. If rape's involved you need to talk to the police. Or certainly your parents, friends."

"My parents, no way. It would kill them. My friends from high school are all scattered and I can't talk to the friends I have in the Army. They might have to report it. Police. You're kidding. No way. He's my cousin."

"I'm sure there's someone."

"Please. There isn't. Don't you think I've been through everyone?" Her voice was high and trembling.

Ben waited, not knowing what to do. She looked at him, waiting for an answer of some kind. He had no idea what to say. He took a big breath and got out, "Of course you've thought of everyone. Sorry."

"We always used to kid around and sort of flirted. He's ten years older than I am and so it seemed harmless. You know. He's my cousin and he's married. Last time I was home, he was home too. We bumped into each other at the Fourth of July party at Maggie's house. He said he'd never had a chance to take me out for a drink since I turned twenty-one and he really wanted to do that. He said he knew this neat beach bar in Fairfield so we went there the next day. I don't drink a lot and was really feeling it after a few drinks so he suggested we go for a walk on the beach. He started telling me about all the problems he was having with his wife Nancy and how she didn't understand what it meant to him to be in the service and he was glad he could talk to me about it because I was in the service and I understood. We started to hold hands and at one point he kissed me. I know I shouldn't have but I was a little drunk and, shit, I was lonely too. I haven't had a real boyfriend since high school. So we kissed and then we went back to the bar and had a few more drinks. He asked if it would be okay if we stopped at his parent's place on the way home for a minute because he needed to pick something up. I said sure."

Her lower lip was quivering and Ben had to strain to hear her. "No one was in the house. We kissed a few more times and one thing led to another. We wound up having sex. I'm not on the pill. Nancy is. He didn't have any condoms and I sure didn't, but we just went ahead anyway. I told him he had to pull out, that I didn't want to get pregnant. He said he would. But he didn't. I could tell when he was ready and I shouted at him to stop but he wouldn't. I tried to push him off, but he wouldn't get off. So now I'm pregnant and he's back at Fort Irwin in California." Nora was barely getting the words out through the tears.

Ben didn't say anything. They kept walking. She stopped crying after a couple of minutes and continued, "I can't afford an abortion. I'm broke. I was stupid and bought a new car when I enlisted so I've got this big car payment every month and there's no way I could care for a baby alone in or out of the Army and the Army sure won't want me. They don't cover abortions and I'm Catholic anyway. Even if I decided to get an abortion I couldn't afford it. Where am I going to get five or six hundred dollars?"

"From him." Ben's answer was a declaration, not a question.

"Yeah. Like he's got it and what's he going to tell Nancy."

"I don't know. Seems to me that's his problem."

"Yeah right."

"I'm serious. Look. I don't know if you really want an abortion or not. You keep saying 'I'm Catholic' but then you start talking about abortion. All I'm saying is that no matter what you decide to do, he's got some responsibility here. Remember, he raped you."

"Sort of."

"You keep saying sort of. You told him to stop and he didn't."

"Yeah. I told him to stop."

"So he damned well knows what happened. I don't get this 'sort of.' Have you talked to him about it?"

"Sent him an email. He emailed me back and told me to get an abortion, said I started it and I wanted it as much as he did and I couldn't expect to get him worked up like that and stop, especially if he'd been drinking. Then he said that if I wasn't pregnant we wouldn't even be talking about whether he got off me or not."

"Nice guy."

"Yeah, but the truth is he's probably right. If I didn't get pregnant we wouldn't be talking about it."

They kept walking. Ben tried to collect his thoughts before he said, "Look I don't know what you want to do, but if you want an abortion and you want him to pay for it, or even half of it, tell him that's the way it's going to be. He's not going to want to risk his wife finding out or the rest of the family."

Nora didn't say anything. They had reached a park. Ben motioned towards the entrance. Nora picked up on his cue and they crossed the street entering the park.

"What would you tell me to do if I was your sister or something? Do you have a sister?"

"Come on, that's not fair. But yeah, I do have a sister."

"Why isn't it fair? Couldn't she make a mistake?"

"Of course she could. I just meant….."

"What?"

"I just meant every situation is different and people believe different things."

"Are you Catholic?"

"Not really. Sort of was."

"Is your sister?"

"I think she's sort of the same place with that I am."

"What would she do?"

"Honestly, I don't know what she'd do." Ben was surprised. He really didn't know what Molly would do.

"What would you tell her to do?"

Ben paused: "I'd tell her it was her decision."

"But what would you want her to do?"

"What do you want me to say? I feel like you want me to give you an answer of some kind." He was wishing he had never agreed to talk to her.

"Never mind."

"Maybe we should head back." He turned around and started back towards the diner. She walked a couple more steps and then turned around to follow him. She used longer strides to catch up.

She was firm with him: "You'd tell your sister to get an abortion. I can tell."

Ben didn't say anything.

"You would. Wouldn't you?"

"I told you what I'd say."

"Yeah, but I can tell. You'd want her to."

Ben stopped and looked at her. He looked at her like he was just seeing her. He could see where the tears had stopped. He saw how red the rims of her eyes were. He could see she was tired – very, very tired. He kept looking at her: seeing her, inhaling her. When he began to talk to her, he knew his voice had changed. It was his brother voice, the one he used when Molly was in trouble and she needed him and she wasn't just being stupid.

"I'd tell her it's a hard decision but one that only she could make."

"That's it?"

"No."

Nora looked at him waiting. He knew that she wanted him to say something. Ben waited, wanting to make sure he got it right.

"I'd tell her to try to imagine it was five years from now. Depending on the decision she made, what would her life be like five years from now? How would she feel? What would she regret? What would she feel good about? Looking back, how would she feel about her decision?"

Nora stayed still. They just looked at each other. There was no time.

Two teen aged boys maneuvered their skate boards in and out of the pedestrian traffic in the park. One quick push after another followed by long glides. Slight shifts in their hips changed directions, first one way and then another, coming close but never hitting the people walking. The wheels made a steady low hum. The skateboarders weaved past them.

"Shall we?" Ben asked softly nodding towards the diner. Nora didn't say anything and began walking. Ben followed her as far as his car.

Sarah at Chanukah, 1993

> "Don't let the light go out
> It's lasted for so many years."
> Peter Yarrow, 1983

Peter and I talked most of the way to Denver
About our children, our mistakes, our age,
And the other things of middle-aged men
Meeting for the first time through the
   accident of seat assignments.
He would go on to Telluride to relax
While I went to Snowmass to teach and ski.
We said good-bye at the gate for commuter flights.

Five years before we sat in the front row
Of Temple Israel and Peter sang to you
   one of the only children there,
To make you welcome and because he's Peter.
Seven years later you sang his song
In your school's holiday concert and
Perhaps knew it in a secret way
   the others could not
   because Peter had sung it to you.

It's time now to bring out the Menorah
I bought you in Seattle last year,
Searching with your brother and his wife
To find one that would last you through your years.

You sing the blessing now
  --clear, firm, knowing—
A step beyond the little girl
  Singing with her mother.

You sing alone now
  no longer searching for words
  and add your generation's voice
  to the history of your race.

Unknowing, you bless me with these moments
Which I store in memory.

Creation, Compassion, and Commitment:
Towards A Cosmology of Social Transformation

[The following is from a speech I gave to the faculty of the Institute for Health Care Communication in 2001. In retrospect, I am much more aware of how these three constructs – creation, compassion, and commitment – are core to the person I aspire to be. VK]

A family therapy teacher I once had used to say, "Think along with me." It was meant as an open invitation to consider rather than accept, to be creative rather than compliant. That's the invitation I offer you in these notes: to think along with me.

I simply want to share some thoughts and invite you to think along with me as I do so: no expectation of acceptance and certainly not even the glimmer of a concern for compliance. In fact, with this subject matter, compliance would be completely self-defeating.

We are all aware of leaders who have brought about transformation in our world. We honor them for the responsibility they assumed to make these transformations happen. At one level their efforts are inspiring because of what they sought. At another level, their efforts may sound mundane because of the "grind it out" quality that they have required. Both are real. Both are true. Let me suggest that both the inspirational and the mundane aspects of transforming a social system are cosmological issues. Cosmological – again, I simply ask you to think along with me.

I use this somewhat imposing word deliberately. So let me begin with it: cosmology, the study of the cosmos. It's not a word that we use too often in conversation. For me, the word immediately evokes a sense of wonder, humility, and mystery. I certainly can't deny the existence of the cosmos, but how, though, do I define my place in it?

I do believe that how we think about social transformation and social responsibility is related to how we think about the cosmos and our place as humans within it. Let me get to specifics. In my understanding of the cosmos and of social transformation within it, three elements stand out. I do like alliteration. So here they are: creation, compassion, and commitment. First, some thoughts about creation and society.

Creation

I haven't looked at the Baltimore catechism that introduced me to Catholic Theology in years. Theology takes on, as one task, a consideration of the cosmos. While I haven't looked at the catechism in years, I do remember the question and answer format and that the little green book answered all of the big questions, however satisfying or dissatisfying the answers seem to me now. My memory tells me that the first question was, "Who made me?" Now that's a cosmological question if there ever was one. The answer, as I recall it, was "God made me." It then went on to tell me that He (applying the male pronoun to the divine was not an issue back then for the authors of the Catechism) made me to love and serve Him in this world and be happy with Him in the next. It's amazing how I remember that – more than sixty years later – verbatim. In retrospect, it was very clear to me that creation was God's business and I had little or nothing to do with it.

I don't believe that any more. Now I don't believe that I am God and I can make a cosmos, but I do believe that I, that all of us, are involved in a creative process in this cosmos and that in this way we are god-like, if not God. When I truly ponder our power to create, I feel a tremendous responsibility, one that is truly awesome and awe full. Let me try to explain my thinking.

The socio-biologists claim that some of our actions are hardwired by our biology and that there is very little that you or I can do about it. I didn't create that hardwiring. Some creative power in the cosmos gets credit for that. For example, my fight/flight responses to the perception of threat are probably as hardwired as the use of my fingers to grasp things. At some point we may figure out a way to alter that hardwiring but, for now, I have to learn to live with it. However, what I perceive to be threatening is derived from my life experience, and how I choose to fight or take flight is learned behavior that I can alter. And so I participate in creating both my perceptions and my responses.

Consequently, at an individual level, I am clearly a co-creator with the Great Metaphor that

I'll refer to as She to equalize the gender bias a bit. Now, the minute I accept responsibility for the creation of my perceptions and responses, I quickly find myself with moral and ethical questions because how I see things and what I do affects others. My perceptions and my subsequent actions form patterns. Ultimately, then, I am responsible for the creation of a perception/action gestalt that impacts the lives of those around me. Over time these choices, this exercise of my power to create, have regularity to them. I can call this pattern of choices my character, for lack of a better word. I can choose to be a courageous or a cowardly person. Clearly, at an individual level, I am creative or co-creative. When I step back and ponder that by making choices, by being cowardly or courageous, I am creating my character, and I find myself filled with amazement at the fact that we are all doing the same thing.

What, then, about society? I believe the same process takes place at a social level. Sociologists and anthropologists claim that in our interactions with others, the ways in which we live socially, we must accomplish certain tasks that are universal (a short hand for saying hardwired) and that these tasks will always be attended to. For example, we will protect our tribe (however we establish the boundaries), we will educate our young so they can survive, and we will tell stories that explain our cosmos to ourselves. And yet we are all aware of the tremendous variance that exists in the "how" we go about doing these tasks regardless of how central or mandated by cosmological forces beyond our creative abilities they are.

We, you and me, create this social variance. We, or our ancestors, created it, and, in this country, outlawed slavery. Please note, we have yet to do away with it, but we did make it illegal. We created and ended human sacrifice to a variety of gods. Another note: I sometimes wonder if "isms" and religions don't continue with a program of human sacrifice, only now we call it war or terrorism. We have created, and now wonder if we can we end, racism. We have created, and make some effort to end, gender discrimination and gender violence. We have created, and at least are aware of, a class society that bestows upon a very small number of people – those who are in this room among others – most of the world's riches. And, of course, let us not forget one of our biggest creations: war and its close cousin, genocide.

If we live and interact with others, we can not avoid being part of this creative process. This is what gives truth to the old saying from the sixties, "If you are not part of the solution, you are part of the problem." As we know, both fortunately and unfortunately, that is all too true. By our very existence as social beings we create the societies in which we live: our marriages, our families, neighborhoods, communities, our countries, and, yes, our professions. When we are silent, we consent to what is and implicitly state, "It ain't broke, so there is nothing to fix." Silence is always perceived as consent. Or, by our actions, often involving tremendous courage, we transform our cosmos. At times we create a new nation and found it on principles which we express in a bill of rights, at other times we simply carve out time to spend with a sick friend – just to be there. We are always creating our society. There are very few givens.

For the past three decades I have been concerned about the creation of the social system that provides health, healing, and comfort. Much of my energy has gone into the professional development of the clinicians who work at the core of this system. And sometimes I despair at the system we have created, either by the consent of our silence or our own, less than admirable, actions. Some stories convey my despair. This is from *Kitchen Table Wisdom* by Naomi Rachel Remen (1996). It describes the social system we call medical training and professional development at work. She writes:

> As a pediatric intern, I was a secret baby kisser. This was flagrantly "unprofessional." I was careful not to be discovered. Late at night, under the guise of checking a surgical dressing or an IV, I would make solo rounds on the ward and kiss the children goodnight. If there was a favorite toy or blanket, I would be sure it was close, and if someone was crying I would even sing a little. I never mentioned this dimension of my health care to anyone. I felt the other residents, mostly men, might think less of me.

One evening as I was talking to a patient's father in the corridor, I glanced over his shoulder and saw Stan, my chief resident, bend over the crib of a little girl with leukemia and kiss her on the forehead. In that moment I realized that others, too, might be struggling to extend themselves beyond an accepted professionalism to express a natural caring. Perhaps there was a way to talk about these things, even to support one another.

One night when we were waiting to be called to the operating room for a C-section, I told Stan what I had seen and that it had meant something important to me. Although we were alone in the doctors' lounge, Stan denied the whole thing.

We dropped the subject in embarrassment. For the rest of the year we worked together, thirty-six hours on call and twelve hours off. We became trusted colleagues, good friends, and even occasional drinking buddies, but we never mentioned the incident again.

Stan's integrity was almost legendary. He would never have fudged a piece of lab data or said he had read an article when he hadn't. But he would have had to step past our entire professional image and training to admit his heartfelt reaction to that little girl. It was impossible then. It is barely possible now. Expressing caring directly rather than through a willingness to work a

> thirty-six hour day or spend long evenings keeping up with the medical literature and newest treatments transgresses a strong professional code. It was just not professional behavior. I stopped kissing babies then. It did not seem worth the risk.
>
> In some ways medical training is like a disease. It would be years before I would fully recover from mine (61-2).

She did recover. That is the good news. She believes it is barely possible now. That is also good news. But everyone in medical education could tell a similar story and we could probably use an experience from this past year. And that is the bad news.

By our silence or our action, we created this social system and we can create a different one. Our ability to create and re-create is our birthright as humans. That is our place in the cosmos: to create the social systems in which we live and leave behind for our children and their children. Our freedom is not boundless. We are co-creators after all. But when we do it well, we are glorious.

We can never, though, become creators until we confront the two *isms* that stifle our creative efforts: nihilism and cynicism. I am worried about current challenges to our creative roles that come from these two sources.

Nihilism, the belief that nothing matters, is a creeping, crawling sickness of the spirit that can consume us before we are aware of its presence. Several years ago I had the privilege of working with a fascinating group of people to develop a human sexuality curriculum. It was a joint project of the United Church of Christ and the Unitarian Universalist Association. The chair of our committee suggested we spend some time reading the lyrics of music that were popular with teens at the time. This was almost twenty years ago. We did so. It sensitized me to an emerging nihilism that I hoped would disappear. Today, I am aware, instead, of the escalation of this nihilism in the popular culture of our young people, and it scares me.

Young people have always been rebellious and celebrated the outcaste and the wanderer. What I am referring to, though, is new. In part, it is the acceptance and expectation of gratuitous violence. In part it is the flirtation with self-mutilation in order to feel something, anything. What concerns me the most is the silence of the adult world except in fleeting calls for censorship. I worry about our creative spirit.

I don't see that nihilism in the medical world. I am thankful for that. But I do see a growing cynicism; a caustic, corrosive, going to get better, no one cares, and I had better watch out for myself because no one else will. The cynicism is often expressed in a kind of whining. This is surprising given that it comes from the most highly educated, wealthiest profession in our society.

Simply, everything we create is not good. Even though I am not sympathetic to the whining, I do believe that there is a parallel tragedy being enacted in which patients are called consumers who are serviced by providers. The unfortunate choice of language, consumers and providers, comes from a system in which the goal is to reduce costs to increase the bottom line to make the stock attractive. The impact: physicians have been demoted and patients are objectified.

Money and medicine have always had a contentious relationship. The horror stories of completely unnecessary surgeries, extensive Medicaid fraud, and refusal to treat non-paying patients pre-dates the dominance of managed care in the United States. In those less than admirable times, physicians were in charge. Now they are not, unless they are stock holders or administrators. Does this mean that single payer systems produce less cynicism? A recent study comparing care in a variety of European countries found that Spanish doctors were scheduled for eight minute consultations. Instead, they spent ten minutes and worked extra hours to play catch up. Medicine and money are contentious, whether it is keeping taxes down, pushing stock up, or scamming the system.

The cynicism we hear today is that of the practitioner. We listen to the impotence. The good old days are resurrected. That is the way it was. This is the way it is. Who knows how it will be? Some social commentators have noted that everyone today is vying for a position in a hierarchy of victimhood, including physicians.

We know that this contentious relationship between money and medicine will always be with us and finding the balance will always be difficult. Either/or, thinking won't work.

My crystal ball is as cloudy as everyone else's about the future, and I certainly don't have any elegant solutions to this conundrum. But I do know that the creative spirit will always encounter nihilism and cynicism. To thrive, the creative spirit must circumvent these distractions and, instead, be rooted in things that matter and a belief in possibility. Because the medicine/money tension is, perhaps, a universal one, we cannot let it distract us from our work. We can't indulge ourselves in cynicism and fight for our place in the hierarchy of victimhood.

And so we come to the need to carve out our own vision of what is possible, to celebrate our birthright as creators. What do we want to create – through our silence or our action? Because, one way or the other, we will create.

When it comes to the relationship between clinician and patient I could give you my laundry list of what I think matters in the relationship. And, being a cockeyed optimist, I always think that my laundry list will come to pass. Let me suggest just two items. I will dare to use the word create.

Politicians love coining slogans. In my lifetime I have lived through the "new frontier," "the great society," and more recently George W. wanted me to live in the "compassionate society." These are all short hands, sometimes with, sometimes without, substance. Recently we have heard a lot about putting an end to "social promotion" in public schools -- not advancing children from one grade to another simply because they are a year older. Instead, the argument goes, provide afterschool and summer programs to assure that the kids have the skills necessary to do the work of the next grade. Not necessarily a bad idea, if the programs are provided as promised.

Shamelessly, I am going to borrow a piece of the school metaphor for my vision and engage in a little of my own coining of terms. I want us to create a system of medical education that no longer accepts scientific promotion. I'd like to end scientific promotion in medical school and residency training –let's stop advancing students and residents from one year to the next simply because they have mastered a scientific body of knowledge or put in their time. Instead, let's make movement from one level to the next only possible when the learner has demonstrated interpersonal as well as scientific competency. I would add to that. Movement from one level to the next is possible only when the learner has demonstrated both interpersonal and scientific integrity. We have the knowledge and the tools to do this today. Do we have the will, though, to transform the system of medical education, to re-create it, in this dramatic a fashion where interpersonal competence and integrity become as central to the practice of medicine as scientific matters? Or, if we need a slogan: Let's end scientific promotion.

Number two. I want us to create a system in which the scientific paradigm is not the only way of knowing within the practice of medicine. I want to restore the scientific paradigm to its rightful place as one of many ways of knowing and being. Let me give an example here so you understand what I am and am not advocating. Recently one of my colleagues attended a conference by one of the leaders in the evidence-based medicine movement. The speaker implied that when evidence was clearly for or against something, it did not need much discussion with the patient. Or, shared decision making is only critical in the absence of clear-cut evidence. My colleague called me the next day, outraged.

Philosophy is a way of knowing. Ethics, a branch of philosophy, is a concern for "right action." Do we truly allow knowledge into our world that is not supported by the scientific method but may be supported by other ways of knowing? Do we want to demote shared decision making and patient autonomy to an occasional event because a series of studies have given us probabilities? Can we have only one way of knowing? Do we throw out ethics as way of knowing and only allow science as our point of reference?

And what of the simply human? Can that chief resident Stan bend down and gently kiss that child only if he has scientific studies to support his action? Is it only science that makes medicine a profession? I hope not. At Columbia P&S Rita Charon uses literature to move students into a deeper contemplation of the world in which they are entering. This is tragic: not that she does it, but that her work is so notable because it is so rare.

My desire is not to ignore, end, or limit the scientific in the medical enterprise, but, instead, to create a social system in which many ways of knowing are acknowledged and supported.

These, then, are but two of the elements in my vision: first, that interpersonal competence and integrity become essential components of the system through which we develop clinicians. In my world it becomes unthinkable not to do this. And, second, in my vision, many different ways of knowing are welcome and celebrated.

I believe both of these are possible and both matter. My laundry list could go on. The items don't all relate to the balancing of scientific inquiry and mastery to other modes of knowing and mastery. We are creators. If we choose to create a system that incorporates these two elements, we can do so. Again, I only ask that you think along with me. More importantly, I would ask you to embrace your birthright as creator. What kind of social system are you creating on your first, second, and third day? You do get to rest on the seventh.

Compassion

We can create garbage: the shadow side of our creative power. That's why creativity is not enough. What was that senior resident, Stan, doing when he bent down to kiss that child? I believe this to be the second essential component of a cosmology of social transformation: compassion. What we create must be grounded in compassion or we can misuse our creative powers and find ourselves creating and living in elitist systems that foster inequity and disenfranchisement.

Compassion is such a powerful carrier of meaning that it needs definition. My own understanding has come from my schooling and from witnessing what I understand to be compassion. More recently, I felt compelled to study the work of a renegade Catholic theologian, a former Dominican priest, by the name of Matthew Fox. He is, by the way, now a married Episcopal priest having been kicked out of the Catholic Church for his teachings. Yes, I am attracted to mavericks.

I was taught very early on that compassion was action. Being Jesuit trained, I came to know something of Thomistic philosophy. Thomas Acquinas taught that compassion was not pure feeling but included moral decision making and action, doing something based upon the decisions you make. It was linked to justice making. To illustrate, we have Luke's story of the good Samaritan. It has been used over and over to define compassion:

> He had compassion and went to him and bound up his wounds, pouring on oil and wine; then he set him on his own beast and brought him to an inn and took care of him.

For Matthew Fox, the contemporary theologian, compassion is not pity; it is celebration of our shared humanity. It is not sentiment; it is justice making and doing works of mercy. It is not private, egocentric, or narcissistic; it is public. It is not merely personalistic; it is cosmic. It is not ascetic detachment or abstract contemplation; it is passionate and caring. It is not anti-intellectual; it seeks to know and to understand. It is not religious; it is a way of life. It is not a moral commandment; it is a flow and overflow of the fullest human and divine energies. It is not altruism; it is self-love and other-love at one with each other. (Fox 1979)

Fox quotes psychologist William Eckhardt: "Compassion is moving towards equality, guided by the assumption that human beings are equally human" (11).

Fox again: "Compassion is a spirituality of meat, not milk; of adults, not children; of love, not masochism; of justice, not philanthropy. It requires maturity, a big heart, a willingness to risk, and imagination…Compassion moves beyond the beginning stages of spiritual searching to a fuller stage of dialectical living that experiences both cosmic contemplation and local pain and then gives birth to alternative healing of that pain" (17).

And it is joyous and we celebrate together.

I want to emphasize the celebration and the joy. Rachel Remen invited Stan to do that and he was unable. Instead, constrained by the social system that we have created, he had to deny his compassion for that sick child, his oneness with her, the openness of his heart to her. And, as a consequence, he sealed himself off. And, Remen, his intern, stopped kissing babies. When we exile compassion, we do just as Remen says: we create a social system that is sick. We need not only to assure that compassion guides our creativity and our actions, we need to celebrate compassion even in the simple sharing conversation that Remen offered Stan.

She tells another story. Another personal one. She writes:

Airports, even familiar airports, are very difficult to negotiate alone when you have lost a good deal of your eyesight as I have. Boarding a recent flight out of San Francisco, I sank into my seat with relief and belted myself in. I was seated at the bulkhead on the aisle. The window seat was occupied by an elegant older man. There was an empty seat between us. Looking to escape the tension of the past half hour, I put my purse on it, took out a murder mystery, and began to read. When lunch was served an hour later, I was deeply engrossed, the book inches from my nose. We were given a salad, a bagel, and a pint container of yogurt. Times have changed.

Continuing to read, I tucked into my plate until my seatmate gasped in dismay. Turning my head slightly, I saw that he had upset his full container of yogurt onto the floor, spilling it on his shoes, the rug, and part of his overnight bag. He was looking out of the window. I waited for him to take some action, but nothing happened. Looking down again, I saw that he was slowly drawing back his right foot, the shoe covered with yogurt, until it was almost hidden under the seat. I could now see his left foot clearly. His ankle was swollen and a metal brace emerged from his shoe. His left leg was paralyzed.

The seat belt was still on. I reached up and rang for the flight crew. No one responded. Some time later when the drink cart arrived, I indicated the floor and asked the stewardess for a towel. Before I could say anything more, she went ballistic: "There are four hundred and fifty-two people on this plane," she snapped. "I'm doing the best I can, you'll just have to wait." Her defensiveness baffled me. We looked at each other in silence. Then I realized that it simply had not occurred to her that I was a participant. "If you bring me a wet towel, I will be able to get that up," I said quietly. She hesitated and I wondered if she had heard. Then she raised her eyebrows, turned on her heel, and brought a towel. After the cart had passed us, I looked again at my seatmate. He continued to look fixedly out the window, his left foot motionless, his right hand hidden under the seat.

"I used to love to fly but I find it difficult now," I said, and I told him that in the past few years I have had trouble seeing. Still looking out the window, he told me that eight months ago he had suffered a stroke and now had no feeling in either of his arms from the fingertips to the elbows. Yet he had flown halfway across the country to spend some time in the home of his son. He was

> *speaking almost in a whisper and I leaned toward him to hear. "Since my stroke I am incontinent," he said, "I have to wear a diaper." I nodded, marveling at the choreography of this chance seating arrangement. "I have an ileostomy," I said. He turned to look at me and asked what that was, and I explained that my large intestine had been surgically removed and I wear a plastic appliance attached to the side of my abdomen to collect my partially digested food. I added, "Even after thirty years I am concerned that it might leak. Especially on a plane." After a moment we smiled at each other. Then he looked at the towel I was holding and I looked down at his feet. As we had talked he had brought his right foot out from under the seat, "May I?" I asked motioning with the towel. Kneeling I began to wipe his shoes. As I was doing this, he leaned forward and told me, "I used to play the violin."*

She comments on the episode:

> *More and more, we seem to have become numb to the suffering of others and ashamed of our own suffering. Yet suffering is one of the universal conditions of being alive. We all suffer. We have become terribly vulnerable, not because we suffer, but because we have separated ourselves from each other.*

A patient once told me that he had tried to ignore his own suffering and the suffering of other people because he had wanted to be happy. Yet becoming numb to suffering will not make us happy. The part of us that feels suffering is the same as the part that feels joy (145-8).

Compassion. None of us would question that Rachel Remen was compassionate. She saw, she felt, she decided, she acted. What, though, of the flight attendant? If nihilism and cynicism block our capacity to be creative, what thwarts our capacity for compassion. Fox suggests that there are three forces at work. I think we see them all play out with the flight attendant.

The first is competition. Competition establishes hierarchies. It is an attempt to control. It separates us from others. It establishes winners and losers. As a society, we create rules knowing that competition unleashed can lead to violence on others. What we may be missing, though, is that continuous competition consumes so much energy that winning becomes everything. Competition may cause us to grow blinders so we can't see anything if it is not straight ahead. If we work and live in a competitively limited world, the blinders don't let us see what else is taking place with and to others. By definition, competition separates and creates we's and they's: inclusion and exclusion.

This is hard for me. I am competitive. I was raised to be competitive. Competition also corrupts me. I hope the corruption is not of the kind that leads me to illegal or unethical practices. I do believe, though, that competition leads to a corruption of the self. When I am care-less rather than care-full, too much of my energy goes into success-making which my ego can identify with and not enough into justice-making. A friend of mine once said that he became liberated when he stopped worrying about being brilliant, and tried, instead, to be effective. Fox refers to psychologist Karen Horny (1937). Horny pointed out we become competitive to gain power, prestige, and possessions. According to Horny, we need the power to avoid feeling helpless, the prestige to avoid humiliation, and the possessions to fight our fear of destitution. (Horny 201) The irony, of course, is that it is compassion, not competition, that allows us to join our brothers and sisters and to become truly filled and joyous in the process.

Our flight attendant, though, lives in a competitive environment that is more interested in serving drinks than helping a disabled man – willing to sacrifice the one for the many. Her other passengers had to come first. She didn't even have time to listen.

The second enemy of compassion is compulsion. Fox writes:

> There is something about compulsiveness that blinds one to all but one direction and renders one dangerously single-minded. Like lemmings dashing to their death, compulsive persons or cultures hear only one cry, one call, one direction, one

ideology. This exclusivity which is common to so much driveness is so simplistic, so one dimensional, and so cold to others' pain and joy that the possibility of compassion is thoroughly banished. It results in a fundamental lack of imagination that is easily threatened by creative people (79).

All our flight attendant could see was the drinks to be served. Compulsively, anything that interrupted that task was unthinkable. One of the difficulties with many management systems is the insistence on compulsion and the accompanying banishment of imagination and creativity. The imagination to consider the "other" and the creativity to respond are criticized as "soft" or "not business-like."

The third block to compassion is dualism. Dualism is the complete separation into either/or. Our flight attendant could not see that Rachel Remen was a participant. Her dualism only allowed for crew and passengers. Consider the way dualism separates doctor and patient. Roles are essential in our lives, but they need not be inflexible. And we best be careful to understand what are the essential elements and what are mere artificial trappings.

To be compassionate we must embrace a dialectical consciousness in which we are aware simultaneously of our connections and our differences – this is the essence of Buber's "I Thou" construct.

One of my heroes, the family therapist Sal Minuchin, teaches that the first task of the therapist is to "join" the patient. To find the simple, common experiences of our existence that connect us together. Later we can differentiate into the role specificity that brought us together. Note that I say differentiate, not disconnect. Differentness can help; disconnectedness cannot.

As Fox teaches us then, competition, compulsion, and duality can all interfere with our capacity to use our creativity in compassionate ways. As Rachel Remen shows us, joining our neighbor, not hesitating to act amidst the messiness of being human, and allowing ourselves to see and feel suffering is joyous.

We can always ask ourselves: is compassion central to the exercise of our creative power? Or, as Carlos Casteneda asked through his Yaqui Shaman many years ago: "Does this path have a heart?"

Commitment

Creating a society that is rooted in compassion is not easy. And that's why social transformation takes commitment. As Robert Frost ended his poem about the darkest night of the year: "…I have promises to keep, And miles to go before I sleep; And miles to go before I sleep."(Frost 1923)

The promises are the easy part; it's the bloody miles that make it hard.

Margaret Farley is a Christian ethicist. She teaches at the Divinity School at Yale. She wrote a very important book: *Personal Commitments.* (Farley 1986)

Yes, personal commitments. We are accustomed to using the word with personal relationships. In her book Farley demonstrates how essential commitments are in all aspects of our lives: relationships, work, ideas. She writes:

> Commitment, then, entails a new relationship in the present – a relation of binding, and being bound, giving and being claimed. But commitment points to the future. The whole reason for the present relation as "obligating" is to try to influence the future, to try to determine the actions we intend and promise. Since we cannot completely do away with our freedom in the future…we seek by commitment to bind our freedom, though not destroy it (18).

Commitments, Farley writes, *often begin in feeling.* I believe that social transformations of the kind that I am addressing today are filled with emotion. For me the experience often begins in outrage. I worked in the South during the sixties because segregation, discrimination, and racism made me mad. It was only later that I began to fully understand and appreciate what was at stake. One of the leaders of the civil rights movement in Mississippi, Mrs. Fannie Lou Hamer, used to say, "I'm sick and tired of being sick and tired." You commit to act when you get sick and tired of being sick and tired.

I have three daughters. I will never know the subtle shades of gender bias they experience on a daily basis. There are occasions, though, when that bias raises its ugly head to a level where even I recognize it, and then my emotional experience is one of outrage. Behind the anger and the outrage, though, there is the connection to these young women in my life. I am a father. I have promises to keep. If my emotions are working, the anger transports me and I experience my love and I am moved to act. If my emotions don't work, I deny myself and these young women and sit on the sidelines of their lives like a spectator. Social transformation brings compassion and commitment together in acts of love. And we need to experience and express the commitment because as Farley writes:

> Commitment is our way of bringing freedom to bear on unpredictable changes in our feelings; it represents our attempt to make love endure, to prevent the kind of process which would dissipate love and obscure the self we want to be (39).
> …..
> Commitment is our way of trying to give a future to a present love. It depends upon the power of the past (promise) to influence the present (fulfillment). It aims to strengthen us, so that our love will endure through time; to assure us so that we can trust within

time; to integrate love so that one day's fears do not threaten another day's desires, or one year's weakness overwhelm another year's strength (40).
…..
The ultimate meaning of the promise I make today can be clear only at the end of my life and its end will be different because of the promise I make today (42).

I believe that it is through commitment that the self is revealed and develops. As the Unitarian minister Jack Mendelsohn was fond of saying, "If you would know me, then know my commitments."

In Mitch Albom's wonderful little book *Tuesdays with Morrie,* we are invited to meet a sociology teacher in the last days of his life, dying of Lou Gherig's disease. (1997) Morrie was a teacher, a great teacher. And he chooses to end his life honoring his commitment to teach. Rather than giving in to his disease, his home becomes open to friends and former students. He makes a commitment to experience his journey into death fully and to teach others about it. In telling what happens on the Tuesdays he visits with Morrie leading up to his death, Mitch remembers another conversation when Mitch was Morrie's student at Brandeis. Mitch writes:

One afternoon, I am complaining about the confusion of my age, what is expected of me versus what I want for myself.

> *"Have I told you about the tension of opposites?"*
>
> *"The tension of opposites?"*
>
> *"Life is a series of pulls back and forth. You want to do one thing, but you are bound to do something else. Something hurts you, yet you know it shouldn't. You take certain things for granted, even when you know you shouldn't take anything for granted...A tension of opposites, like a pull on a rubber band. And most of us live somewhere in the middle."*
>
> *"Sounds like a wrestling match,"* I say.
>
> *"A wrestling match." He laughs. "Yes, you could describe life that way."*
>
> *"So which side wins?"* I ask.
>
> *"Which side wins?"*
>
> *He smiles at me, the crinkled eyes, the crooked teeth.*
>
> *"Love wins. Love always wins."* (40-1)

Farley talks about three things interrupting commitment: conflicting desires, the loss of the original vision, and a loss of presence. We are all familiar with the conflicts that enter our lives, especially when we are competent and people call upon us for many things – Mitch's wrestling match. Several years ago I was developing leadership programs. I was struggling with some concepts and brazenly called Williams College to talk to James MacGregor Burns, the author of the book *Leadership*. He was on sabbatical and the young man running the switchboard gave me professor

Burns' home number. I called. He was most gracious. And then he taught me. He said, "Vaughn, I enjoy the subject of leadership, and I think you are on the right track, but I am focused right now on finishing my work on the political history of the United States and I am not sure when, or if, I will ever get back to leadership." When ,or if: He let go of the conflict. By the way, he did get back.

The vision which forged the love can go out of focus. Mistakenly, we may think it is more in focus. We wind up saying things like, "Now I see what this movement, this person, this university, this job, is really like." We see trees now. Up close. When we made the original promise, we saw the forest from a distance and, in our vision, it was beautiful, and worthy, and good.

Our commitment can be threatened by our loss of vision, by our inability to embrace how messy life is, including us. And sometimes we get so close that our ability to see is distorted.

One of my favorite places to be is sitting on a bench in a room at the Art Institute in Chicago looking at Le Grande Jatte. But Seurat's wonderful picnickers enjoying their Saturday afternoon lose their very being and become dots of paint if I leave the bench and get too close.

I can also lose my ability to be present to my commitment. It may be that it is time to move on. But it may be that I am so trapped in the present that I can't be present. I act and I observe, but I am not there. I become the spectator, numb to others and probably to myself. A gestalt teacher I had used to say, "The purpose of therapy is not to make you feel better; it is to help you to feel." As Farley writes, "Commitment is our way of bringing freedom to bear on unpredictable changes in our feelings…" How, then, do we renew? How do we find fidelity and avoid betrayal?

For Morrie the dark night of the soul was the dread of having to have to ask someone to, as he said, "Wipe my ass," when he could no longer do it. When the time came, he was able to stretch time, his time, to being a child again: dependent, trusting – and he went on teaching. He tells Mitch:

"Mitch, it's funny," he said. "I'm an independent person, so my inclination was to fight all of this – being helped from the car, having someone else dress me. I felt a little ashamed, because our culture tells us we should be ashamed if we can't wipe our own behind. But then I figured, *Forget what the culture says. I have ignored the culture much of my life. I am not going to be ashamed. What's the big deal?*

"And you know what? The strangest thing."

"What's that?"

"I began to enjoy my dependency. Now I enjoy when they turn me over on my side and rub cream on my behind so I don't get bed sores. Or when they wipe my brow, or they massage my legs. I revel in it. I close my eyes and soak it up. And it seems very familiar to me.

"It's like going back to being a child again. Someone to bathe you. Someone to lift you. Someone to wipe you. We all know how to be a child. It's inside all of us. For me, it's just remembering how to enjoy it.

"The truth is, when our mothers held us, rocked us, stroked our heads – none of us ever got enough of that. We all yearn in some way to return to those days when we were completely taken care of – unconditional love, unconditional attention. Most of us didn't get enough.

"I know I didn't."

I looked at Morrie and I suddenly knew why he so enjoyed my leaning over and adjusting his microphone, or fussing with the pillows, or wiping his eyes. Human touch. At seventy-eight, he was giving as an adult and taking as a child (Albom 115-6).

Morrie found a way to be present, to honor his commitment to experience and to teach his final lesson.

Farley writes, "Commitment is love's way of being whole when it is not yet whole; love's way of offering its incapacities as well as its power."

And for those of us trying to transform this system we call health care, we must continuously renew our commitment to this work. Sometimes it is lonely work. We live in a system filled with the cynicism that inhibits creativity. We live in a system in which competition, compulsion, and dualism thwart compassion. We live in a system in which conflicting values, myriad details, and feeling trapped in the present cloud our commitment. We probably all have colleagues back home who, like the horse in Robert Frost's poem:

> … think it queer
> To stop without a farmhouse near
> Between the woods and frozen lake
> The darkest evening of the year.

Is this time in health care the "darkest evening of the year"? I doubt it, but there is not a lot of light, either. I think we do know why we stop, and why we start again, and again.

> …we have promises to keep,
> And miles to go before we sleep,
> And miles to go before we sleep.

And we must fill these miles with creativity, compassion, and commitment. If we do, I believe we will transform this system we call health care. As Morrie said, *love always wins*.

Thank you for thinking along with me.

References

Albom, M. Tuesdays with Morrie. New York: Doubleday, 1997. Print.

Farley, M. Personal commitments: Beginning, keeping, changing. San Francisco: Harper & Row, 1986. Print.

Fox, M.. A spirituality named COMPASSION and the healing of the global village humpty dumpty and us. San Francisco: Harper & Row, 1979. Print.

Frost, R.*Stopping by woods on a snowy evening.* New Hampshire. New York: Henry Holt, 1923. Print.

Horny, K. The neurotic personality of our time. New York: Norton, 1937. Print.

Remen, R. N. Kitchen table wisdom. New York: Riverhead Books, 1996. Print.

Getting Even

People fill their time in different ways after a divorce. If they have a job, they can swim in endless hours of work, and more work if their occupation lets them.

As a nurse, that was easy for Joan. She put in hours at the hospital and then hours doing private duty and then more hours going over claims for an insurance company. Although she was making a lot of money, the work solution wasn't successful for too long. The years of nursing wear and tear on her knees and back sent pain signals to her brain that let her know that, at sixty-five, the hospital and private duty work solutions were no longer viable and the claims work bored her. She could have had her knees replaced, but they weren't that bad yet, and the thought of recovering in a rehabilitation facility, because there was no one at home to care for her, was, the way she saw it, an expensive sign of failure. So she retired from all of it.

Retirement, though, was too different. It was an icy stream that took her breath away and seemed to grab at her heart, squeezing it and sometimes scaring her. There was no getting out of the stream. It carried her deeper and deeper into a frigid whirlpool that never ended. She knew she had to crawl her way out and do so dramatically and quickly or she'd be stuck there forever.

First, she sold her house and bought a condominium in the town where her sister Marilyn lived. That felt wonderful. She and her sister had never been close and the two of them were anxious to build a bond that had never been present before. The ten years that separated them in age had always seemed an insurmountable difference.

Moving four hundred miles from where Joan had been living also was a welcome change. She approached it with the same anticipation that she felt when the start of daylight savings time announced the coming of summer. She was looking forward to learning a new town and exploring the surrounding areas.

Two weeks after she moved, Marilyn up and died from a heart attack. Marilyn smoked and was overweight and Joan always warned her, but they were sisters and Marilyn was not about to pay any attention to her younger sister, even though she was a nurse. There was to be no bonding.

The frigid whirlpool returned. It quickly took away any warmth that she had felt with the move and the plans for becoming close to Marilyn. This time she had a slightly better understanding of the vortex, though, and did not wait as she had before. Marilyn had deceived her and abandoned her and Joan knew, as one knows when one is getting a cold, that she could either get sucked in or break out of it by making even more changes.

She went to the library and registered for a card. That completed her move. She took out a book on retirement and the perils of retirement and made a list of the things she must do. There were a lot of suggestions and she winnowed them down to a few that felt congenial.

She became a joiner. She joined a church. She joined leagues and committees to preserve things, beautify things, teach things, and do whatever the town seemed to need doing.

Clubs came next. They were like leagues but were a bit more insular: she joined a book club, a photography club, and a gardening club.

Subscriptions came after that: she subscribed to the regional theater, the local orchestra, and even an amateur theater group that was very, well, it was very amateurish. She numbed herself with a steady dose of activity that tamped down any and all questions of how she had gotten to be sixty-five with no children, no grandchildren, two divorces, one cat, and a paid for condominium in a town that she barely knew but had moved to because her older sister Marilyn lived there.

After Marilyn's funeral, Joan went for a long walk on the beach. She didn't cry. She didn't scream. She had given up on both a long time ago. She thought about getting drunk, but that felt too adolescent. Instead she decided to get even. There was no one in particular to get even with, so she decided just to get even without knowing exactly what that meant.

The first thing she had to do, though, was stop going to church every Sunday. It was a new parish to her and no one would miss her if she wasn't there. Somehow a life of getting even and going to church on Sunday didn't fit together and, even though her life felt a bit chaotic, Joan did not like things that did not fit together.

Driving home from the beach she felt freer than she had in a long time. She was going to get even. She had to do it without making anyone know that she was the one getting even. That was okay. She didn't feel any intense need for recognition. Her soul had lived in a hardened state for so long that recognition wasn't a consideration. Besides, she didn't yet know who or how or when the getting even was going to take place, so how could anyone else know it was her? When she started, though, she would use her nursing training to make sure she made no errors in either judgment or execution. She would use everything she had learned over the years about errors in systems and how to avoid them. She would make W. Edwards Demming, the now dead guru of quality improvement, proud. Hers would be acts of getting even that would stand up to the standards of all quality measures. The hospital had trained her well.

She chuckled to herself: no malpractice suits for this girl.

She doubted there were any books about getting even when she began her internet search. But she knew there were lots of books in which people were hurt, and lots of television shows and movies she could study. The more she thought about it, the more excited she became. With her settlement from the last marriage and her judicious investing of ten percent of all of her wages for forty years, she had enough money so she didn't have to work and, more importantly, she didn't have to worry about money. In fact every month there was quite a bit left over after she paid for her basic necessities. She lived frugally and always had, so getting even could be a full time occupation if she wanted. She smiled just thinking about it.

Getting even would take some time so she might have to quit some, but not all, of her activities. That reminded her: she had to keep up the activities where people saw her smiling. They didn't have to know what she was smiling about. She quickly rethought her decision about church. That was a place to be seen as a happy person who smiled all the time. Who knew, getting even might even make her happy.

Joan was used to doing everything according to the book though. So the absence of acceptable protocols for getting even disturbed her. One late evening on the internet, however, she became ecstatic. She discovered several sites that would get even for you. She had never considered getting even as a business. She spent a full hour on "Payback.com." They emphasized revenge. That was close to getting even but not quite what she had in mind. For a price they would send things from dead fish to nasty emails – anonymously of course. But you had to pay. What was useful, though, was the wonderful classification of wrongs that could be addressed.

She was also wrong about the books. There were several. She was intrigued by *Getting Even: The Complete Book of Dirty Tricks* by George Hayduke. She ordered it from Amazon. Actually she ordered the whole series of books by Hayduke. She also ordered *The Revenge Encyclopedia*. By the time she was through, she had spent close to two hundred dollars and felt well on her way to becoming a *getting even expert*.

II

That night she slept better than she had in years. She had just buried her sister, but the truth was that the potential bonding was probably a fantasy. Joan really didn't like Marilyn very much anyway. When she woke up the next morning everything seemed nicer than any morning had for the entire spring. The coffee tasted better than it had the day before. The flowers in the hanging pot over her balcony were the brightest they had ever been. She wondered if this is what some of her Evangelical friends meant when they said they were born again.

She was still in a quandary, though, about the very nature of getting even. The idea faded in and out of focus as she sat on her balcony, looking out over the parking lot of the condominium complex.

Why had they put the balcony on this side of her unit? It was stupid. Really stupid. It was nice having that clarity. She wasn't disappointed by the stupidity this morning the way she had been every other morning. Being disappointed by stupidity was a thing of the past. In her born again state she was clear that whoever the architect or developer or builder was that made the decision about the balcony simply did stupid things and didn't care about the people who would eventually live in the condominium. She wasn't irritated or angry. She was simply aware of the stupidity and lack of caring. The awareness wasn't taking anything away from her enjoyment of the moment. Maybe, she thought, getting even was that simple. You just had to be aware of stupidity and uncaring and then make the perpetrator suffer as he or she caused others to suffer.

In her mind a formula started to develop. It was like a chemical interaction. Mix stupidity with lack of caring and you had a fertile ground for getting even. Perhaps it was really that simple.

She went inside and picked up the notebook and pen that she kept next to her telephone and brought them out to the balcony. She sat down and started writing down the formula: stupidity plus lack of caring equals a reason to get even. She still had to figure out the get even part. Suffering was clearly part of it. That was where the equal sign belonged. Algebra. That was it: stupidity plus a lack of caring causes suffering so it must be balanced by an equal amount of suffering. More clarity emerged. She had to become an expert on suffering and how to cause it. She wrote down, "Make them suffer," and underlined it three times. Instantly she knew what was wrong with Payback.Com. Their revenge tactics caused inconvenience and irritation, but not suffering.

Talk about being born again, she thought. All of those years as a nurse she had worked to mitigate suffering. Now she was going to cause it. She squirmed with delight just thinking about it. She thought about how easy getting even really was. Stupidity plus uncaring made you guilty because the two together caused people to suffer. Getting even was simply balancing the equation. It was making things even, making the algebraic equation come out right. There had to be an equal amount of suffering on both sides of the equal sign. *Oh my*, she thought, and clapped her hands.

Her reverie on getting even was interrupted by the rumbling of the diesel engine that propelled Mitch Blackman's oversized pickup truck. It was very noisy, very tall, and had four wheels in back rather than two. As usual, he pulled it into the visitor's lot and took up two spaces. His wife's car was in their driveway and the garage was reserved for Mitch's shop. Although he was flagrantly disobeying the condominium regulations, he was on the board of the association and chaired the buildings and grounds committee which no one else wanted to do. Consequently, although people complained about Mitch's parking behavior, no one dared to challenge him about it since Mitch controlled how fast and how competently repairs might be made on your unit should you need his assistance.

When Joan's neighbors, the Whiteheads, gave an engagement party for their niece, they approached Mitch and asked him to take up only one of the spaces. Perhaps he could park the truck in his driveway and his wife's car in the visitor's spot. He told them to mind their own business and people could walk in from the road. His response made the rounds of the swimming pool and, while people commiserated with the Whiteheads, no action was taken. This was a clear case, Joan decided, of where someone should have gotten even but didn't. Perhaps she might rectify the omission.

That evening she went on the internet and learned about tires and how they operated. She hadn't realized that one could purchase a very small instrument that could remove the inflation valve from a tire and that all of the air would immediately escape.

She kept exploring. She was falling in love with the internet. It gave her all of the information that she needed. Her time in front of her computer was growing exponentially and she felt like she had just made a new friend who was completely responsive to her. She discovered that if one search engine failed her, she could go to another and then another. Eventually she would find what she wanted. For example, deflating the inside rear tires would probably not be noticed until a heavy load was put on the truck and that could possibly break the axle. Joan was getting excited. The videos on tire maintenance showed her exactly what she would have to do.

The internet told her that three towns away was an excellent auto supply store. A forty-five minute drive guided by her GPS system got her to the store, and she had no difficulty finding the tool she wanted. She also found something else: stick on signs that said, "Don't Park Here!" The clerk assured her that the glue was very powerful and difficult to remove. He said it could take fifteen to twenty minutes to remove just one sign. Joan bought ten.

Joan's next concern was the Whiteheads. She was concerned that Mitch would blame them for anything that happened to his truck. She made it a point the next day to visit the pool at the same time the Whiteheads usually did. It was easy to get into a conversation about summer plans and what activities her neighbors had that might cause them to be out of town for a weekend or longer and who would know they had left. The information was easily forthcoming and, within thirty minutes, Joan had the perfect weekend. She would have to wait a few weeks and she would have to spread the word in casual conversation so Mitch would be sure to know that they would be away, but she knew she would be able to do that.

The time dragged slowly. People continued to do what they did on a regular basis. Mitch never changed his obnoxious parking habits and Joan turned herself into a little busy body, talking about summer plans, and she made sure that Mitch knew when the Whiteheads would be away and even where they were going. No, Joan wasn't going anywhere that summer. With the pool and all, she was content to stay put during the summer. After all, the pool was one of the things that attracted her to this particular complex. She was, though, thinking about learning how to play golf.

Finally the day came: Sunday morning. The Whiteheads were away for a long weekend, four hundred miles away. She was relying on a couple of sentences from a television show to choose the time for her venture. Michael Westin on *Burn Notice* said that three to four in the morning was the time that most people were asleep, or very sleepy, and the least likely to notice anything.

She put her dark coveralls on. She made sure her tire instrument was in one pocket and the stickers in the other. All of the lights in her house had been off for hours. She was using nothing more than a small pinpoint Maglite. She was very quiet going down the stairs from her second floor unit and left the front door slightly ajar so she wouldn't have to use her key to get back in.

She quickly walked to the visitor's parking lot and rolled under the pickup truck. It was high off the ground and easy for her to do. She quickly found the tire valve for the left inside tire. The instrument worked perfectly. In seconds the tire was empty of air and she replaced the stem. It wasn't really flat because the outside tire now did all the work. She rolled over to the right side and repeated the procedure. A second tire was soon deflated. She tucked the instrument into her pocket, buttoned it up, and turned off the Maglite.

Rolling out from under the truck, she pasted two signs on the driver's window, two on the passenger's side, two on each of the rear side windows, and two more on the back window. It took less than three minutes to cover all windows.

Quickly she returned to her unit, went inside, quietly locked the door, and went upstairs. She felt her way out onto her balcony and went out. She stayed close to the wall that separated her unit from next door. She peeked over and looked around. No lights were on. She heard nothing. She went to bed and giggled to herself. She didn't fall asleep until six o'clock.

Mitch's shouting woke her up. It was a nonstop stream that combined curses and threats in close to equal proportion. People were looking out from their balconies or front windows to see what was taking place.

An hour later, he was still hard at work using a scraper and a bowl of hot water and a sponge removing the "Don't Park Here" signs. The cursing had diminished to only occasional outbursts. The threats had become more pronounced and Joan worried a bit about the possibility of Mitch finding out it was her but quickly dismissed the fear as irrational.

Mitch was bent on retaliation, but he didn't know who to retaliate against. Around midday, when many of the cars were gone, he moved his truck and parked it horizontally in the visitor's space so it took up close to four of the spots reserved for non-residents.

That evening the condominium's telephones and cell phones began to earn their keep, and it wasn't long before a conference call of the board was in progress. Mitch was not included in the call. The president tried every reason he could think not to be the one who talked to Mitch, but everyone agreed that he was the only one who Mitch might listen to without a major confrontation. He doubted it, but finally agreed that he would take on the task.

The president was in luck. Mitch was not home when he courageously rang the doorbell, having also agreed that he would have the conversation in person. Mitch's wife answered the door and it took the president but a mere ten minutes before she agreed that she would park in one of the visitor's spaces and Mitch would use their driveway. She warned the president that Mitch would probably resign as chair of buildings and grounds, but the board had already discussed that and was willing to accept the eventuality.

The talk at the pool that day was all about Mitch and the brave soul who dared to do anything. Joan listened and only spoke when she could reinforce what someone else was saying. Inwardly, she was repeating her "getting even" formula as though it were a mantra. "It works," she said to herself quietly. "It really does work. This is a force for good."

On Monday Mitch had to pick up an extremely large load of lumber for a project he was beginning work on in the next town. On the way out of the lumber yard his truck went over a speed bump. Without the support of the inner tires on the real axle, he heard it break, followed by the sickening grinding sound of metal on asphalt.

Mitch never mentioned his mishap to anyone at the condominium. That night he talked to his wife about moving. Joan never knew what happened to the truck. It didn't matter.

III

Pleased with her getting even formula, Joan spent the next few months looking for opportunities to put it to good use, but after the episode with Mitch, she wanted to find something worthy of the formula. She also found that she needed to occupy a bit more of her time, so she began to volunteer as a parish nurse and to spend a few hours each week helping out in the rectory doing some secretarial work. Convinced that she was on a mission for good, any scruples that she had previously experienced about participating actively in the life of the parish had disappeared. She was now recognized by the more active members of the congregation and, with her efforts and smiling demeanor, she was thought of as one of the star volunteers, and people talked about how lucky they were that she has joined their parish

Joan enjoyed the work of parish nurse. She basically checked in on people when they were recovering from serious illnesses, surgeries, or were homebound. She didn't have the responsibilities that she had at the hospital and didn't have the physical demands of moving bodies and being on her feet for up to twelve hours at a time. She would check to make sure people were taking their medications, but she was not responsible for dispensing them.

The leader of the parish nurses at Our Lady of the Sea was about Joan's age but appeared, at least to Joan, to be quite a bit older. She had retired several years ago with some kind of vague disability that members of the parish mentioned but were unaware of any specifics other than that on occasion Margaret would not be able to fulfill her duties and others would have to cover for her. That was how Joan discovered that Margaret was stealing opiates from her patients.

Joan was very diligent about assuring that her patients were taking their medications. Consequently she would count the remaining pills in their medication bottles. One week when she covered for Margaret, she kept discovering inconsistencies between the prescription dates and the remaining pills in the patients' medication bottles. The differences for each patient were small, one or two tablets perhaps per patient, but when combined, they added up to a sizable number of opiates and benzodiazepines – all controlled substances.

Joan concluded that Margaret was stealing medications to either address her own needs for drugs or to sell them. Given the frequency with which older nurses had become addicted to various drugs until more recent and more stringent controls over medications were put in place, Joan surmised that Margaret was a drug addict. No longer working in a hospital, being a parish nurse, gave her access to drugs with little chance of being caught. And, while questions might be raised about an individual patient, the likelihood that anyone would ever see the pattern was very unlikely. *Very clever*, thought Joan, but what should she do about it? Margaret's behavior was clearly appropriate for the application of the "Getting Even" formula, but how could she go about it while remaining invisible?

After a great deal of thought, Joan decided she would wait for several weeks after Margaret had resumed her duties as leader of the parish nurses and was again visiting her own patients. That would provide enough temporal distance so she would not be suspected as being the one providing information to the authorities or, in this, case three authorities: the police, the state licensing bureau, and the State Department of Health.

Reporting the theft and suspected drug abuse or selling of drugs was relatively easy. MIS Defense Products had several devices available to disguise one's voice and even change a female voice into a male voice. The cost of a device was minimal, only twenty-four dollars. The one she selected was delivered in a matter of days.

Pay phones were becoming dinosaurs, but there was one outside the hospital and that seemed like a good place to call from so none of the authorities would be able to track the telephone call back to Joan who was now going to sound more like a Jim than a Joan on the recording that the police would have.

Joan decided to only report on two families. She hoped that would be sufficient for the authorities to detect a pattern and to proceed on their own to discover the other patients who Margaret visited and stole from. She was right.

Almost a month from the day, she made her call, Monsignor Deavey called the three other parish nurses together for a private meeting in the study of the rectory to tell them the news. Poor Margaret had been arrested for stealing. He was shocked, and he informed them that Margaret, *poor thing*, had a history of drug abuse that she had developed while working as an intensive care nurse. She had managed her addiction for years, but, when her husband died, her need resurfaced and, because her role as a parish nurse gave her easy access to drugs, she found herself once again quieting the pain of her loss with the illicit medications. He asked them to pray for Margaret and to provide her with love and friendship during this time of need.

Joan was quivering with rage as she left rectory. She had fully expected the Monsignor to be grateful that the bitch had been found out as a thief and drug addict who was potentially putting patients in harm's way. Instead, he was asking them, *he was asking her*, to be loving and kind, and even to befriend this woman who was a disgrace to her profession.

Joan's fury was barely contained as she rushed home, ran up her stairs, and into her condominium unit. The bottle of Scotch that currently sat on top of the refrigerator had moved with her three times without being diminished. That night it befriended her. And the next. When she called the secretary at the rectory, she told her that she was so upset over what had happened to Margaret that she needed a few days without seeing patients.

On the third day she woke up and realized that she hated Monsignor Deavey. He was in opposition to justice. He had thwarted the formula. He wasn't ignorant of the need to get even; he was against it. Compared to Mitch and Margaret, he was a monster. Perhaps, though, the formula was wrong or was simply incomplete. The situation with Margaret and Monsignor Deavey suggested that it was more than simply stupidity and uncaring that led to the need to get even. Certainly neither cared about the cost to patients nor the possible danger that Margaret had put them in. On Margaret's side, perhaps, it was stupidity. She thought her pilfering would never be discovered. Monsignor Deavey was not being stupid, though; he was knowingly interfering with the need to get even. He was consciously replacing "getting even" with empathy. There was no justice in that.

IV

Joan increased the time she spent working in the rectory. During the day she would do simple secretarial tasks. She mailed out the newsletter, she kept track of the calendar, and she even helped with some cleaning. At night she worked on her formula. She considered incorporating "intention" into the formula. This led her to questions of motivation. She considered the impact of the act on the victim. She played with one variation of the formula after another and tried to be reasonable in her deliberations, but she acknowledged to herself at times that Monsignor Deavey was an enigma to her. However, her feelings about him were not. She eventually returned to the original formula and simply classified Monsignor Deavey as stupid and uncaring when it came to justice.

That calm did not last long. Overhearing three telephone calls changed everything.

In his early seventies and too vain to use a hearing aid, the Monsignor was loud on the telephone in his study; Joan could hear every word he said if she was working next door in the administrator's office.

She was finishing up her work on the weekly newsletter when she heard Monsignor Deavey call the prosecutor and ask for mercy for Margaret. She couldn't hear what the prosecutor said, but it was clear from the Monsignor's side of the conversation that he was listening intently and using his priestly warm voice in pleading Margaret's case. She was afraid the Monsignor would hear her snap the pencil she was holding, but he kept right on talking about Margaret's virtues.

It was when he made the second call to a bail bondsman that Joan's fury took hold and any pretense of applying a reasoned formula to the situation was no longer possible. He had gone from being a compassionate priest to an accomplice in a crime as far as Joan was concerned.

The third call confused her at first. It was to someone called James. The Monsignor's voice was different still. He was intimate, even a little afraid. He was trying to assure James that using some of the minister's discretionary fund to pay the ten percent of the twenty thousand dollars for the bail would not delay their plans. Margaret would show up for her appearances and pay them back over time. Yes, they would still have enough money for their trip to Myrtle Beach later in the year. Yes, they would meet in the usual place next Tuesday.

He was sorry that the Bishop had turned James down when he requested retirement next summer. They would work something out. The call ended with, "I love you, too."

Gripping the edge of the desk with both hands, Joan did not have to use her imagination to understand what she had just overheard. No wonder Monsignor Deavey was willing to support and help Margaret out: he was just like her. No, he was worse, far worse. He was pilfering money from the minister's discretionary fund to pay for his vacation with his gay priest lover. This went way beyond stupidity and not caring. This was true evil; this was betrayal.

Joan didn't stop to chat with the cook when she left the rectory through the kitchen. The cook said good-bye to her twice. Joan didn't acknowledge her either time. She just went home and locked her door. She didn't leave home for a week. It took that much time to solidify her plans. She needed another few days to buy what she needed and to learn everything she needed to know about it. She carried out her plan the following weekend.

V

Joan liked being back in a hospital environment, especially since she didn't have any duties other than to go to the silly group meeting every day and see the young psychiatrist once every two weeks to check on how she was doing with her medication. It had been eight months since her trial. It was really only a formality because the prosecutor and the judge were in agreement with her lawyer that jail was not a good place for her.

None of them understood. She was tired of trying to make them understand. When that horrible Monsignor Deavey died from the arsenic she had put into the sacramental wine, she was sure everyone would be delighted. She arranged for him to die during Mass on Saturday night. She told the parish everything about his lover James and the pilfering from the discretionary fund in an anonymous letter she slipped into the weekly newsletter the following Monday.

The members of the parish didn't care. The parishioners knew about James. They knew about the vacations. They loved Monsignor Deavey and didn't care about those things. He loved them; they loved him. He was their priest. When she got no reaction to the letter, she realized how deeply the evil had reached into the parish and that she would have to go public. She didn't want to but she had no choice.

The following week at Mass she stood up at the end of the innocuous homily and lectured the parishioners about Monsignor Deavey. She told them why it was just that he die because he had betrayed them, but to her astonishment they directed their horror at her, not him.

The morning nurse was nice and she brought her the pad and pencil she was allowed to use for an hour every day as long as it was under supervision. Joan kept working on the formula. She kept trying to make it account for everything that had transpired. It was very difficult, though, and when the psychiatrist had more than the allotted ten minutes to check her medication, she tried to tell him what she was working on, but he did not seem to pay attention. When he did respond, he was placating and his interest was disingenuous. At first she wondered if he was stupid and uncaring, or just uncaring. After a few months she concluded it was both.

Daffodils

"It's the day I cut the first daffodils
And put them in the dining room.
It changes every year.
I never know when it will be."

It was not the answer I expected when I asked,
"What's your favorite day of the year?"
I got the question from my sister
Back when I was shy
And didn't know what to say
When you meet a girl you want to know.

That was forty-seven bouquets of daffodils ago.
I told my granddaughter the story one more time
As she bent to place the vase upon
Her grandmother's grave.

Standing back
I watched and wondered,
Did I ask enough questions
Through the years?
What was …
The second best day of the year?

I Wish I had My Camera With Me

I've said that multiple times. You may have, too. My children, and now my grandchildren, probably think it is the remark of an old, or at least older, person, because they are always taking pictures with their smart phones. They always have a camera with them. I have one of those, too, but it can't do what I need at times when I really need a camera, a real camera, one that can zoom and focus and capture lots of information whether it be on film or in pixels.

This past Tuesday I wished I had a real camera with me as I drove up our driveway. It was a hot day about one o'clock in the afternoon. The sun was high in the sky.

On our front lawn we have a white Adirondack chair with an equally white foot stool. From them you can see our pond just beyond the pine trees. It is lovely there on the mostly green lawn in front of our Cape Cod house. Classic look. On this particular afternoon a black cat had tucked itself into the shade cast by the chair – in order of ascendency it was green grass made greener and darker by the shade, lounging black cat, and the shelter of a white chair. The contrast was so stark, so perfect, I wished I had a camera with me. I would have needed a good camera, though, to capture what I saw. What I saw, though, was well beyond these elements of grass, shade, cat, and chair.

I remember teaching poetry to high school students many years ago. They all wanted freedom of course, the energy of adolescent rebellion racing ahead of their wisdom. I used to begin a consideration of the discipline of poetic structure by teaching the ancient Japanese form, the Haiku. The Haiku is usually formed with two contrasting images in a 5, 7, 5 sound form. But it doesn't have to be. I always began with a poem by William Carlos Williams you might remember from when you were in high school:

> *So much depends*
> *upon a red wheel barrow*
> *glazed with rain water*
> *beside the white chickens.*

That afternoon it all depended upon the black cat beneath the white chair. Meaning in a moment. Meaning beyond the capacity of narrative language. The meaning found in a poem, a painting, or, yes, in a photograph.

I think that is what all of those moments are when we say, "I wish I had my camera with me." It is the artist in us knowing that a simple retelling of what we saw in narrative form can't capture our experience. It is our aesthetic impulse reaching out to record the elements that gave such intense meaning to that moment. We want that moment. We want to hold it close and never forget it. We wish we had the camera with us.

The Truth is Enough

I don't remember when Ed Lynch said this to us or what the context was that prompted it. I also don't remember whether he said it to me directly or to the group at large. I will never forget it though. It was one of those moments of epiphany that will never leave me.

Ed was my Gestalt trainer at Southern Connecticut State University. As a teacher and therapist he was special, gifted, unique, and a royal pain in the ass which is true of every special, gifted, unique therapist and teacher – perhaps royal pain in the soul would be more accurate. His affirming and loving presence made the pain tolerable, most of the time.

"The truth is enough." So simple, but did I believe it? It calls for a very big leap of faith. No minimization; no exaggeration; no deceit; no obfuscation. All things I am quite expert at. Over the years I have become increasingly convinced, a true believer. I do believe the truth is enough. Living it is still problematic, of course.

I use to refer to the political season as the "silly season." I don't anymore. The stakes are too high. As I talk to people and hear their fears and see the consequences of political decisions, none of it is silly to me anymore. Consequently, I wish, that Ed Lynch could train all politicians and scramble around in their souls until they emerged believing that, "the truth is enough."

It would be easy for me, a card carrying liberal, to aim Ed's vision at Republicans, tea partiers, and conservatives, especially in 2012. But that would be in error. Politicians who I am supporting, who I want to get elected, are as guilty of minimization, exaggeration, deceit, and obfuscation as the other guys. Okay, maybe not quite as much, but every time the fact checkers rip into President Obama I wince. I want to scream, "Why don't you just speak the truth. It is enough. Honest."

Similarly, when Elizabeth Warren makes absurd claims about her Native American heritage and why she identified herself as such I want to scream at her. I almost did once. It was a campaign event. Local. Not very big. Small enough so I could have a few moments one-on-one. It was before the Massachusetts convention in Springfield and some of the papers had been urging her to address her claims head on. I mentioned it to her and she laughed, "That's a big nothing. No one is paying attention to that stuff." She didn't get it. For weeks the Boston Herald kept it up. "Liawatha," was bestowed upon her as a nickname. It was a big something as I knew it would be.

Will I vote for her? Of course I will. Send money? Yes. Done. But there is also an ache that won't go away. I do want to hold "my" candidates to a higher standard than the other guys. I want them to believe and struggle with Ed's dictum that the truth is enough. I can't change the other guys, but maybe, just maybe with enough emails and opportunistic conversations, I can get my team to have a little faith.

Hear Him Out

He is the modern mercenary
Schooled in the liberal tradition
Of the nineteen sixties
Educated and disillusioned by the Peace Corps
He has fought the major wars of his generation:
    for civil rights
    for the rights of farm workers
    for the rights of women
    for the rights of gays
And against the wars in Viet Nam and Iraq

Some criticize him and call him a poverty pimp
With loyalty to no one cause
Merely angry at millions of parents
Substituting for his own.
Embarrassing to his ex-wife
Unacceptable to family and childhood friends
He goes from agency to agency
As new wars replace the old.
Victory is a forgotten hope
As grants move in and quickly disappear.

Often he waits beyond the board room doors
For wealthy wives and business men
To decide which wars he'll fight,
What risks he'll take,
What people to reach
Before they climb into expensive cars

Until the next month's meeting
With their talk of the role of board and staff
And the difference between policy and operations.

His first heroes are long dead—
Taken down by assassins, never replaced.
Now the wars are games without songs
In which survival is long term funding
In a battle backed by government and corporations.

And still he speaks.
Hear him out.
Hear him out.

Why Liberal Religion Will Disappear

Unitarian Universalism, and its proclaimed Liberal Religion, will all but disappear fifty years from now. There are two reasons for this: growing secularism in Western culture and a reluctance to articulate a religion that responds to core questions of human existence.

Unitarian Universalism (UU) is not alone in facing extinction. There is also much hand-wringing within the mainline Protestant denominations in response to the diminished number of people making their way to Sunday services. Until recently UU congregations were holding their own, barely. That is no longer the case. They are now experiencing the same slippage as other mainline denominations. As within the mainline denominations, UU congregations are concerned about the financial consequences of a declining membership. The emergence of part time ministers is a growing trend. Membership and church buildings are both aging. Young people leave, never to return.

There is a lot of talk about the unchurched, now labeled as "nones," and why the unchurched folks of a liberal mindset are not beating down the doors and filling the UU pews to overflowing. The somewhat arrogant statement, "They are UUs and just don't know it," continues to enter conversation with the regularity of a dirge drumbeat at a funeral procession.

I believe Liberal Religion, and most UU congregations, will disappear within the next two generations. Underlying this assessment is a hope. The hope is that Liberal Religion will become a movement that will not simply survive, but will thrive. To achieve this, I believe will require a revolution.

The Unchurched

Western societies have become increasingly secular. In industrialized countries modernity has beaten religion as the dominant cultural force. This has been developing over decades and has escalated as communications and travel have shrunk the world, especially the Western World. This change has several facets.

First, the expectation that one belongs to a "Church" and attends religious services of some kind has continuously diminished. Today one can say with no threat of social sanction, "I am spiritual, but not religious," or, "religion doesn't interest me," or "religion is at the heart of the world's problems." Such expressions one hundred years ago would raise eyebrows, fuel gossip, and, fundamentally, cause the status of the speaker to diminish in the social hierarchy of the listeners and the larger community. Historically, there was social pressure to belong to a church, whether you believed or not. Today, that pressure is significantly diminished – unless you are running for President of the United States.

Second, "religion" has failed the test of creating societies that are consistent with the espoused values of the religion. More specific to Unitarian Universalism, UU congregations are similar to the congregations of most mainline Protestant congregations in that Sunday morning is often the most segregated hour of the week. In addition, classism is alive and well and obvious from the selection of music to the vocabulary of the preaching. When pushes are made to become more inclusive, racially and educationally, a significant number of congregation members become irate and argue that it is up to others to find them. "Unitarian Universalism is not a proselytizing religion," is a mantra for some. Or, they will argue they do not want to "dumb down" the denomination. The language is more polite than this, but the message is clear: UUs like their classism.

Third, there are myriad opportunities in most communities to pursue interests that foster and support one's commitments to social action, spiritual development, and intimate community. One doesn't have to go to church to sign a petition. It is simple to do it online through MoveOn.Org, Credo, or any number of social action groups.

If I want spiritual nourishment in a Buddhist frame, I can go to Krapala on the East Coast, Tassajara on the West Coast, or the local Zen meditation center. Or, I can take myself out on a nature walk alone or with others. I can also read any number of "spiritual" authors and listen to a variety of meditation tapes.

Secular society offers a wide variety of opportunities to form community, intimate networks of friends. As an example, Kaiser Permanente offers new mothers parenting classes. Bonds that are formed during these classes often continue for years afterwards. Clubs abound as do fraternal organizations like the Moose Lodge.

To view the unchurched as deprived of community and opportunities for social action and spiritual growth is delusional and an exercise in wishful thinking. UUs had best retreat from this fanciful image of what secular society has to offer. This is not to suggest that every unchurched individual has managed to successfully negotiate a package of disparate elements to address all of these needs. Certainly one thing that UU churches, especially the larger ones, can and often do provide is bundling. However, most UU congregations are small and the notion of merger is not on the radar screen of most congregational leaders.

Finally, both Unitarianism and Universalism developed as oppositional movements. Understanding the function of this history is critical. Both movements became a home for those who found it difficult, if not impossible, to accept the creeds of the dominant Christian denominations. Because societal norms proclaimed, "Thou shalt belong to a church," both Unitarianism and Universalism provided a vehicle to satisfy the societal norm without the discomfort of stating beliefs and engaging in practices that were antithetical to the questioning views of the congregant. Both denominations filled a need and created a unique niche.

However, without the societal norm to belong to a church, an oppositional frame cannot succeed when there is nothing to be opposed to. The non-creedal flag is only attractive to those who have been immersed in creedal religions. Is it any wonder that so many new UUs come from Catholicism? And the ones who do come were practicing Catholics as opposed to the majority of Catholics who rarely attend Catholic services. Simply, opposition to the creeds of other faiths has no power in an increasingly secular society.

Nevertheless, the unchurched still show up at UU churches to be married, buried, and have their children named. They bring with them good rental income for the congregation and fees for the minister and organist. Since Unitarian Universalism makes no demands on them for things like pre-marital instruction, they can come to UU churches to please their grandparents and the other family members who want these rituals to take place in a church setting. It is clear that some of the old social normative pressures are still at work.

A prediction: rental income in UU churches will continue to decline as grandparents who grew up with those social norms are no longer around.

Today, when a group of new UU's comes together and people are asked to share their spiritual journey, it is usual to hear, "Well, I was brought up_____." In two generations far fewer people will say that.

Envy of the Mega-Church

Liberal Religionists wonder at the success of the mega-churches and often make an incorrect assumption that they are becoming dominant. They wonder how this can be so. First, myth must be separated from fact. The number of unchurched is growing faster than the number who attend mega-churches. Second, the success of the mega-churches is easy to understand: money and music. The mega-churches are often preaching a gospel of prosperity. Services are dominated by inspirational contemporary music with full bands and choirs as opposed to centuries-old music written by dead white men, esoteric bell choirs, and organs. Somewhat cavalierly, one can say that many of the mega-churches (a) put on a good show, (b) support one"s desire to be prosperous, and (c) provide people with moral justification for it.

Looking Under the Hood of Liberal Religion: Is there anything there?

How often does the UU member say to a friend, "As a UU you can believe whatever you want," or "You don't have to believe in anything." Yikes. Talk about invoking radical constructivist nonsense and warping post-modernist thinking into an undisciplined, anti-intellectual nihilism. Liberal Religion, as currently proclaimed by its adherents, is so caught up in its oppositional history that there is nothing under the hood to energize it. No wonder it isn't moving forward.

Many UUs would disagree with the statement that there is nothing under the hood. But what happens when you take a close look?

Unitarian Universalism claims to be covenantal rather than creedal. What happens when that statement is deconstructed? Dictionary definition uses of the word "creed" are, as expected, straightforward: 1. a brief authoritative formula of religious belief, 2. a set of fundamental beliefs; *also* : a guiding principle.

The word "covenant" is a bit more defused. It certainly appears in multiple religious settings. In Judaism it is the covenant between God and Abraham that God welched on: God said He would bless Abraham's descendants making them more numerous than the stars. Nice metaphor, but apparently God didn't account for inter-marriage. The word "covenant" also features prominently in the theology and practices of the Church of Jesus Christ of Latter Day Saints. In the secular world the word covenant is used in a variety of venues from real estate transactions to international relations. When you explore all of the definitions and usages, secular and sacred, you come to the core that a covenant is a "binding agreement."

Both words, "binding" and "agreement," are enormous concepts. Agreement assumes common assumptions and conclusions, alignment of beliefs about a phenomenon. Covenant, then, requires more than similarity; it signals a convergence of viewpoints. Or, "We see this the same way." If a religion is to proclaim to be a covenantal, it best be very careful.

It is true that people can agree on something and have no "binding" attached to it, no commitment to do anything about the agreement. Covenant, though, means commitment "to do." God's blessing of Abraham's descendents was not a free ride. With "binding" comes expectations and accountability.

If Unitarian Universalism is a covenantal religion, is this where we look under the hood – at its covenants? The covenant between Abraham and God certainly is for Judaism, and the Mormons have multiple covenants. Consider the covenant of the UU congregations to affirm and promote:

- The inherent worth and dignity of every person;
- Justice, equity, and compassion in human relations;
- Acceptance of one another and encouragement to spiritual growth in our congregations;
- A free and responsible search for truth and meaning;
- The right of conscience and the use of the democratic process within our congregations and in society at large;
- The goal of world community with peace, liberty, and justice for all;
- Respect for the interdependent web of all existence of which we are a part.

Is this what's under the hood? Sounds like a creed by any other name: "A set of fundamental beliefs." Or are these nice sounding words with no "binding" to either affirm or promote? Are UU members asked to "bind" themselves to these statements? Is this covenant a commitment to action? Or, if Unitarian Universalism is a covenantal religion and you sign on to become a UU, does this mean you cannot believe whatever you want, nor do whatever you want? Does it mean you are forgoing a radical constructivist ideology?

Oops. There is an escape hatch: it is the congregations that covenant to affirm and promote these seven statements, not individual members. So, the radical constructivist is still safe from the clawing hands of being bound to anything.

Wait: let's not go too fast here. Most congregations use a second covenantal statement that is said during the lighting of the chalice, a standard UU ritual. In the congregation I currently belong to the congregation says every Sunday:

Love is the spirit of this church and service its law;
This is our great covenant: to dwell together in peace, to seek the truth in freedom, to speak the truth in love.
And to help one another.

This is our "great covenant": Four actions, four statements of "I must." Keeping in mind that a covenant is binding, the covenant says I am committing myself to "dwell together" with others and do so "in peace." The covenant doesn't tell me much about who I am to dwell with. It also says I must "seek the truth" and do so "in freedom." In addition, I am expected to speak out but to do so in a loving way. Does this mean my lot as a UU is one of continuous seeking and speaking truth rather than falsehood? Finally, I am expected to help others. Who I am to help is not specified.

What does this covenant really mean? Or, is it intended to mean anything? Many religious covenants are between God and the people. In Unitarian Universalism the covenant is closer to secular covenants in that the covenants are among member congregations and among the members of the congregation. If Unitarian Universalism is a covenantal rather than a creedal religion, than one would expect that these covenants mean something. It would suggest that there is a power in these covenants that is central to the congregations and their members. Members are being asked to bind themselves to elements of a covenant as is the congregation.

The seven statements are the only ones that the member congregations have covenanted to affirm and promote. What happens, though, if they don't? Is heresy possible? How is the inherent worth and dignity of all people reconciled with racism and classism?

There is a more basic question though. Can you have a covenantal religion in which everyone is entitled to his or her own truth? The answer in a covenantal religion would appear to be a resounding "No!" The "We" is agreeing to something and is saying we are bound by it. This contradiction establishes a tension within Unitarian

Universalism about what's under the hood, if anything.

A recent scene in a UU Congregation struggling with a mission statement:

> Congregant:*I am concerned about all of these Christians joining the church. It will make us like any other Christian church.*
> Minister*: There are many UU ministers who would identify themselves as Christians. Don't we have to welcome people of different beliefs?*

The Problem and the Solution

Stephen Prothero, in his book *God is not One*, posits that all religions are a response to a core human problem (Prothero 2010). In essence, every religion describes a core problem with human existence and offers a solution to the problem. In his book, Prothero describes the core problems and solutions of the world's eight major religions. Some examples: for Islam the problem is pride and the solution is submission to the will of Allah; for Christianity the problem is sin and the solution is salvation; for Buddhism the problem is suffering and the solution is enlightenment or Nirvana.

Unitarian Universalism grew out of the Christian tradition but left both sin and salvation behind as theological markers. Nothing has replaced them. Liberal Religion has posited neither a problem nor a solution to the condition of being human. The result is that UUs are left to their own devices to construct or choose the central concepts of their individualistic paths. That requires a great deal of work and support. Using the frame of post-modern critical theory, it calls for the willingness to (a) express, (b) reflect, and (c) challenge. It calls for the on-going construction and deconstruction of one's understanding of reality and responses to that reality. UU congregations rarely encourage this work, nor do they have the supports available to develop thousands of idiosyncratic theologians. Consequently, little work is done and members receive no support beyond the tepid "Building Your Own Theology" curriculum and perhaps a lay-led small group ministry program that consciously prohibits challenging one another.

In a strange kind of warping, the result is a non-intellectual religion confounded by the arrogant belief that it is intellectual. The problem is not simply at the congregational level. The ministerial class has not produced theologians of any note for decades. For contemporary theology a UU minister is as likely to turn to a Catholic nun or a Buddhist monk as to a UU.

Looking under the hood, then, one finds neither problem nor solution. In Prothero's construct, Unitarian Universalism is not a religion.

Transformation and Transcendence

Most religions seek transformation and transcendence. How do we transform ourselves to become more realized as human beings? How do we transform the world for our brothers and sisters for this and future generations? How do we transcend day-to-day demands of living to experience the awe, the mysteries and majesty of life – individually and collectively?

In every religion the priestly class is called upon to contribute to the pursuits of transformation and transcendence through preaching, teaching, and modeling. The words "inspiration" and "encouragement" are consistently found when describing this role of the priestly class.

Within Unitarian Universalism only two UU seminaries exist. UU ministers often emerge from seminaries founded on other traditions, usually Christian. While seminaries turn out more UU ministers than the stalled denomination can place, there are few UU preachers who can draw in the unchurched, or retain members, with a vision of transcendence and transformation that answers any core questions of human existence. It is difficult to sort out whether it is liberal religion or liberal religious ministers that have offered an insufficient response to modernity and secularism. A compelling message either doesn't exist, or it is not communicated. The numbers speak for themselves.

What if, though, liberal religion was able to articulate a core problem and a solution? What if liberal religion had a message of transformation and transcendence? What would follow? Unitarian Universalism would likely develop the same accoutrement that Prothero describes for other religions. Unitarian Universalism would not only describe a problem and a solution, it would also have technique and exemplars.

Central Metaphor

The problem/solution axes described by Prothero are often captured in a central metaphor. Religions all use metaphors, and there is inevitably one metaphor that is so central that it is impossible to imagine the religion without it. Try to imagine Judaism without the Torah, Catholicism without the Mass, Islam without praying Salat, Buddhism without meditation, Protestantism without the Bible. These central constructs, whether objects or practices, are intimately associated with the solution to the core problem identified by the religion. These are the vessels of both transcendence and transformation.

Associated with many of these objects and processes is an experience of sacredness and of accompanying vulnerability. Desecration is possible. Ritual is also associated, and sometimes is integral, to the metaphors. Purification rites precede engagement or celebration. There is a "sacredness" communicated clearly and powerfully.

Unitarian Universalism has no unifying metaphor. This is not simply because Unitarian Universalism does not present a deistic face. Buddhism is both non-creedal and non-deistic. Buddhism, however, is very concerned with both transcendence and transformation. Meditation is central to its very being as is the eight fold path. It is interesting that a large number of UU ministers are drawn to Buddhism in the absence of a liberal theology and set of practices that lead to transformation and transcendence. Other UU ministers are drawn to Christianity, and finding a boundary line between their belief systems and those of their United Church of Christ colleagues is often difficult. Still others wonder about transformation and transcendence and find their home in the world of humanism.

Imagine the surprise of the newcomer who is church shopping. In one UU Church the minister is a Buddhist, the UU minister in the next town is a Christian, and one town over he or she encounters a Humanist UU minister.

Unitarian Universalism lacks a central metaphor and similarly eschews any commitment to the promotion of either transcendence and/or transformation, whatever the linguistic or metaphorical system. At times it is easy to question whether UU is, in fact, a religion or a branch of the ethical culture society that has yet to shed its historical protestant garb.

Another Scene, also real:

Congregant: *I consider myself to be a religious humanist.*

Minister: *I am always fascinated with how humanists answer the question of first causes, how all of this began.*

Congregant: *I think science has answered that. It was the Big Bang.*

Minister: *What's your understanding of the Big Bang?*

Congregant: *[Silence.]*

Discipline

All religions have disciplines, what Prothero refers to as technique. The idea is simply that the discipline(s) is necessary to practice the religion and the technique(s) are promoted and opportunities and supports are provided whether it be the bible class, the novena, going on a mission, or the meditation retreat. The secular opposite, the notion that one can be "spiritual but not religious" and not engage in a spiritual discipline, is, by comparison, fatuous.

Spiritual advisors, a common practice in most religions regardless of what they are called, is a role that is missing in most UU congregations. When UU ministers are queried about the discussions that they have in private with congregants, the topics do not differ that much from what the psychologist down the street is talking to his or her clients about. Pastoral care during times of distress and significant transitions is often "non-denominational" in character. It is also being less sought after. This kind of care, though, differs significantly from the role enacted by a spiritual advisor.

Spiritual retreats are rare compared with organizational retreats. When there are retreat centers, as with the Rowe Conference Center – nominally a UU Center – one is more likely to find a workshop being conducted by a poet, a musician, or an artist with no relationship to Unitarian Universalism than a UU minister. One might also find a workshop by a renegade Catholic priest –

now Episcopalian – like Matthew Fox. The idea of a UU retreat master is difficult to imagine.

The "Technique" offered by religions inevitably includes an ethical code, be it the Ten Commandments or the eightfold path of Buddhism. Viewed in this way, the covenant of UU congregations is an interesting mixture of ethical statements, belief statements, and governance statements. No clear technique is described.

Exemplars

For exemplars UUs often cite United States presidents who were UUs, whether or not they were decent human beings, who espoused and lived up to any particular set of ideals. Theodore Parker, also elevated, was a racist. In the UU frame, historical prominence appears to trump principles. What makes a good UU is a question rarely asked.

In almost every religion there is at least one, sometimes more than one, exemplar who was transformed by an epiphany. The epiphany is often related to an awareness of the transience of worldly goods and the necessity to transform oneself into a more whole human being however that is defined. The experience of epiphany and quantum change occurs throughout religious literature and is not confined to a particular religion. Unitarian Universalism is not part of this tradition.

While exemplars in some religious traditions are historical, in others they are not. Contemporary models may be cited and ascribed to a group as is done in Buddhism. These are often the teachers, those who struggle with but who model the techniques leading to transformation and transcendence.

This way of thinking, even acknowledging a need for models, spiritual guidance, or teachers, is foreign to Unitarian Universalism. It raises a truly profound question about what is under the hood other than opposition.

Final Thoughts

Perhaps there is hope for Unitarian Universalism in Prothero's image, that every religion is climbing a different mountain. It may be possible to conceive of Unitarian Universalism as a mountain range. But can you have a religion without the climbing? Can a small denomination of a few hundred thousand offer the supports needed to enable members to climb multiple mountains? And, can you fit a mountain range under the hood of a tiny denomination?

Secularism will continue to grow and, with it, a diminished social pressure to belong to a church. The statement, "I was raised," will not be salient in two generations. As secularism expands, Unitarian Universalism's historical oppositional stance will continue to lose power. The only way that Unitarian Universalism will survive requires a dramatic change in direction, a true revolution. Saying it must move from opposition to affirmation rolls lightly off the tongue, but affirmation of what? Perhaps Prothero's scaffold offers a place to begin: problem, solution, technique, exemplars.

Works Consulted

Prothero, S. <u>God Is Not One: The Eight Rival Religions That Run the World -- and Why Their Differences Matter</u>. New York: Harper Collins, 2010. Print.

Heathrow

I believe I have earned the label of road warrior. Over the past forty years I have traveled more than a million miles – just on American Airlines. They informed me of this last week with a new Platinum Advantage card that says *one million* on it. I never show the card to anyone so it did not seem like much of an acknowledgement. However they did include eight upgrade awards so I will be able to travel first class on one of my trips back and forth to Miami and have two left over. That was appreciated.

I have been to all fifty states but one, Arkansas, and I plan to erase that oversight this fall. Not many people go to Arkansas or live in Arkansas for that matter. And since it comes in last or close to last on almost all categories from household income to college graduates, I don't feel particularly distressed that it will come in last on my states to claim to have visited.

By contrast I am a slacker when it comes to international travel. I have managed to spend time, a great deal of time, in Canada and have been to Mexico and several of the Caribbean Islands and the Bahamas. Across the pond, as the cognoscenti would say, I am limited to Ireland, the United Kingdom, France, Spain, and Switzerland. I have never ventured south of Zihuatanejo in Mexico, west of Hawaii, or East of the Alps.

All of this is a way of saying I have done some traveling and, as such, have come to make judgments about airports. Most Americans will be highly critical of O'Hare in Chicago and Hartsfield in Atlanta. But to me they are gems of efficiency when compared with Heathrow in the UK. The only positive thing I can say about Heathrow is that it has very good shopping, possibly the best of all airports in the world. However, I am not a shopper, and I am certainly not an airport shopper, so I cannot see the shopping opportunities as adequate compensation for the disaster that is Heathrow.

Arriving there this last Saturday night we circled for thirty minutes or so to await our turn in the queue. When we landed we were told that we would have to wait in a land based queue to get a gate. This wait was then going to be extended so we were parked some distance from the terminal and buses were to be provided. The designers of Boeing's 777 did not intend for passengers to have to exit the aircraft by foot. It is a big plane and the door is high off the ground. The stairs are steep and work well for one passenger with their hands free, not for several hundred passengers toting their luggage, presents, children, laptops, and assorted bags of who knows what, in the rain of course, to form still another queue waiting for the buses to take us to the terminal building where we could form still another queue at a gate to now climb up several flights of narrow stairs with all of the luggage, children, etc. Still in the rain.

Once inside, we made our way to the arrivals area and each cold wet traveler was allowed one gasp as they entered the arrivals auditorium to see snaking rows and rows of passengers waiting to be processed by an understaffed cadre of passport inspectors. The sign indicated that if you were "here" that it would be approximately twenty-five minutes before you got to prove that you were a legitimate traveler. One hour and thirty minutes later I was standing it front of an absolutely delightful young man who was chatting amiably with his colleague at the desk next to him about their plans for the following day.

So what does one do while standing in still one more queue at Heathrow? My initial gasp at the length of the line behind me, my anger at being wet and tired diminishing – we were, after all, out of the rain—and my dismay at how long I would be waiting turning into boredom, I decided to observe my comrades at Heathrow as we encountered one of life's minor absurdities. Minor, that is, unless you were traveling alone, had to use the loo, and had no one to hold your place in the queue.

I noticed that there were several ways to advance one's luggage. One approach, favored by the younger set who had backpacks and duffle bags, was the throw and catch up approach. This worked fine in most instances as long as there was sufficient space and the person in front of you didn't stop or move about in an unpredicted pattern. On more than one occasion a "sorry" could be heard as an unsuspecting passenger felt an errant backpack land on their heels.

If the luggage was of the hard variety, but without wheels, the favored approach was clearly the foot push. It was a kind of baggage soccer and worked exceedingly well as long as the suitcase in question traveled in a straight line and did not topple over, still another threat to the person in front of you.

The advanced travelers, of course, had luggage with rollers. These fellow road warriors had little difficulty transporting their luggage along with their selves as they moved through the queue. Some of these vehicles would be piled high in order to avoid having to carry any weight.

One three year old had convinced his parents that he would be quiet if he could ride on his father's suitcase and the two of them had turned it into an interesting game in which the father would push the suitcase back and forth to the delight of the three year old who hung on to the handle while straddling the case itself. This worked wonders until the father accidentally dropped the handle and suitcase with child clattered to the floor. The major difficulty that resulted in screams of pain was that the child did not let go of the handle and so his fingers were underneath the handle as the handle hit the floor with the child's weight on top of it. Enter momma bear into the scenario, scooping up the one very unhappy son, kissing the fingers, cooing at the child while delivering decidedly evil glances at the apologetic father. What had seemed like a good idea at the time had become torment for the family of three and all of the travelers in their vicinity whose ears were being assaulted by the screams of the youngster. Eventually the surprise of the fall dissipated, the fingers still moved without difficulty, and the administrations of the mother brought about a return to normalcy.

The family was difficult classify ethnically or racially. Color and costume were of no use. That was not the case for many of the people in the queue. Both costumes and colors were of enormous variety. The waiting area at JFK was white bread by comparison, and we think of New York City as a melting pot. I remember having the same awakening at the airport in Toronto. Our groupings are simplified. America tends to homogenize people into categories that are reified into artificial distinctions that have no meaning. One of my neighbors in Miami bears a Hispanic surname. Her mother, though, is Italian and Polish and her father is Colombian and African American. Take that, census bureau! Why skinheads and their ilk decry the coming mongralization of the races is beyond me. It is here and has been here for quite awhile. We're just adding a bit of color and some different lyrics.

T-shirts as traveling garb appeared to be confined to those under fifty. Some of them carried messages of what we should do. A young married woman traveling with her husband told us, "Let's get dirty." A forty something year old man, also traveling with his spouse, claimed to be wearing a T-shirt with the international symbol for marriage emblazoned on it. The iconic art work showed a man on his knees before his wife, head bowed, arm stretched out towards her. In his hand he is offering her a credit card. Most T-shirts, though, advertised the names of manufacturers or merchandisers. Champion, Gap, and Nike, were just some of the names that appeared, regardless of the color, language, or remaining dress of the traveler: a grim testimony to the globalization of bad taste. This polyglot gathering brought together by the accident of travel schedules moved easily through the serpentine rows that had been set before them. There were no fights. Other than the initial screams of the three year old of the crushed fingers, there were no raised voices or displays of self importance. People accepted one another and the situation. Certainly resignation was a major component of this good behavior, but, in many instances, people engaged one another in conversation and went beyond the shared frustration of the queue. Business cards were exchanged. Stories of grandchildren were told. Culture and color didn't seem to matter.

I was tempted to make the queue into a metaphor for life in which we are all traveling through space and have limited control over our destinies and who we fall into line with, but I was beginning to get cranky and hungry. Besides, my feet hurt. It was taking too damned long, so I went back to being quietly judgmental and more certain that Heathrow is the worst airport of them all.

Thanksgiving in Little Rock

I did it. I have now been to all fifty states. I am certainly not alone in that feat, but there are not a lot of people who have done it and I was so close, I just had to do it. Arkansas was the last state. It turned out to be a trip worth taking.

The Limits of GPS

I am a very big fan of the Global Positioning System (GPS). I actually own two handheld GPS instruments. One is programmed with waypoints from the Western end of Long Island Sound up to Cape Cod. Every summer a few new ones wind up getting added as new places are visited or new routes taken as I sail those waters on my boat sloop, *Sonas*.

The other one is programmed for the British Virgin Islands. The talk is that you can navigate your way around the islands simply by looking: eyeball navigation. For the most part that is true. But in the middle of a tropical rain squall it's nice to know exactly where you are. Sometimes the coves and bays look very similar and the GPS avoids false starts and the sense of "oops" that every sailor has experienced.

It was Mary Ann's idea to rent one from Avis when we picked up our rental car in Little Rock. I would have relied on maps to find our way around Little Rock, but for ten dollars a day, why not? It got quite a workout in the few days we were there, especially the first night.

Our unit sat proudly above the radio of our rented PT Cruiser, and we followed the precise instructions to the Baker House, the elegant Victorian B&B where we stayed. The Baker House is a truly magnificent place loaded with curly pine woodwork, antiques, and whole rooms converted into baths. It was lovingly built by a highly skilled "Negro" who never lived in it because he was of the wrong color. The historical sign told us the story.

It was evening, we hadn't eaten since breakfast and I was hankering for some Southern BBQ. Our host made a suggestion and found an address in the Yellow pages. After unpacking, we set out. What we discovered though was that our trusted GPS didn't recognize the address our host had given us. However all was not lost. Our GPS had a listing for restaurants; there was a sub-listing for BBQ restaurants. We also had mileage to each of the places that were listed.

We tried a couple of the ones that were closest, but they were both closed. It was Wednesday night before Thanksgiving and the streets of downtown Little Rock were close to deserted even though it was still fairly early. We were even thinking of pizza but decided to try one more place. It was called Sims'. Our GPS liked the idea, and off we went.

One of the limits of GPS is that it doesn't give you any information about neighborhoods. I am not a novice when it comes to rough neighborhoods. I've worked in them on and off and have never had any trouble. But we didn't know this neighborhood other than that it was much poorer than the other neighborhoods we had driven through. Although the stores downtown were closed, here there were people on the street and we knew we had moved through white neighborhoods to mixed neighborhoods to an all black neighborhood. Racial profiling: of course.

We found Sims' and saw people entering and leaving and wondered if we would be integrating the place. As we drove past, we did see a young white couple inside, so we parked the car and headed for the door. There was an interesting sign on the door. It read:

>No ski masks.
>No hoods.
>Keep your hands in plain sight.

Oh, well. And in we went. Of course we were treated cordially and wound up having a wonderful conversation with Ron Blakely, the current owner and cook, about cakes of all things.

About Sims from the take out menu:

*My grandfather and Uncle, George and Allen Sims, and their wives, Estella and Amelia founded **Sims' Bar-B-Que** in 1937. George and Stella established a cafe in the country town of Hard*

Scramble, Arkansas, while Allen and Amelia established a restaurant in uptown Little Rock, Arkansas. Allen and George created a sweet brown barbeque sauce to go along with the tender meat that was prepared with special seasoning.

A guideline was that meat should not be cooked too quickly. They discovered that superior barbeque must be cooked slowly in order to maximize that southern flavor. In this case "slower is better."

*The sauce, seasoning, and cooking technique are the unique ingredients that make **Sims' Bar-B-Que** a unique eating experience. Those unique ingredients have been passed down through three generations and counting. With such a great product, along with unmatched service and presentation, **Sims' Bar-B-Que** will make your event an unforgettable and pleasurable experience.*

Our little event was an unforgettable and pleasurable experience. And if you don't believe us, ask Bill Clinton. According to Hillary it is his favorite place for BBQ in Little Rock. We found that out later. Our host at the Baker House told us that he orders in from Sims' all the time when guests want BBQ.

The GPS, then, is a non judgmental tool, unlike its users. It is one of its limits and I am glad of it.

Rolling on the River

We were two strangers in a strange city on Thanksgiving Day. I had made reservations for us on board the Arkansas Queen. The Queen is a paddle wheel replica that takes people up and down the Arkansas River and offers a variety of programs, from weddings to gospel sings to romantic dinners, and for Thanksgiving. It was sold out.

Everything was included except for cocktails, wine, and beer and all for $35 per person. That included dinner, the trip, the music, and the dancing: at least $100 per person in New York Harbor.

Electric guitar and double bass and standards greeted us and sustained us through the early part of the afternoon with drinks. When the buffet was set up in the middle of the dance floor, the music stopped and the serious eating began.

Every family has its own menu for Thanksgiving and those who would dare to change the menu need protection, especially from the younger members of the family who are often the most insistent on maintaining the traditions. So I missed the pearled onions. However, just about everything else was there, although only pumpkin pie was served: I am an apple pie person.

Birthdays and anniversaries were celebrated and I programmed myself a nod for having completed my journey to all fifty states. One of our tablemates had also completed the journey. He had managed to do so inspecting hospitals. All the members of his party were from Little Rock and were Hillary supporters. We talked about the Clintons and the campaign. They are also Tim Russert fans and were very upset by what they felt was unfair handling of Hillary by Russert during the second debate.

With dinner cleared away, the double bass was traded in for an electric bass and the dancing began. The music and the dancers roamed all over the place but ended up with the Electric Slide and the Chicken for the kids. People danced. They hooped and hollered. It was a party. There was not a television or football game in sight. People sang.

Some things are predictable. The singing and the dancing had to, simply had to, end with Proud Mary. Everybody sang. Creedence Clearwater would have been proud. We knew the lyrics, even the young ones on board knew the lyrics. The band, of course made a minor change which we all picked up on:

But I never saw the good side of the city
Till I hitched a ride on the Arkansas Queen.

We sang our way into the dock. It was a lovely Thanksgiving.

The Library

Coming across the bridge from North Little Rock, you take a left on to West Markham Street which becomes President Clinton Avenue. Along the way you pass restaurants, shops, and the museum store for the Clinton Presidential Library. We were on the trolley that runs from North Little Rock but we had to get off because a traffic accident had blocked the tracks. I loved the quaintness of the trolley but had never thought about the fact that an automobile accident that blocks the tracks has a very different impact on the trolley than it does on cars. The cars just went around the accident.

So we started to hoof it to the library. We stopped before we got there though, captivated by a print hanging in a gallery window. It was a print of Dean Mitchell's trumpet player, one of the series of jazz stamps he produced under commission from the United States Postal Service. We had to go in.

There was a large exhibit of Mitchell's work. There are few things that make me wish I were rich. Art is one of them. I could have bought and bought – I was so captivated by his work. Dean Mitchell is a story teller. What a gift he has and has given us. Unfortunately, even the prints were beyond our budget.

The Hearne Gallery, where Mitchell's work was on display, is a combination gallery and bookstore devoted to the African American experience. It is a special place. It was interesting to see Clarence Thomas's autobiography displayed next to the new Cosby/Poussaint book. Mary Ann bought books for her students. Only budget constrained her.

Still hoofing it, we stopped at the Library Museum Store and I picked up a paperback copy of Clinton's autobiography: *My Life*. My hard copy is still packed away from our last move and I wanted to start reading it while I was in Little Rock. There were some wonderful things in the store including an "I miss Bill" bumper sticker and a "Democrats Only" parking sign. What was interesting was the collection of books for sale. Some I would expect, but others were unexpected. It was clear the museum store ranged from the frivolous to the serious.

The library sits next to the Arkansas River in a park setting and has only one neighbor: the national headquarters of Heifer International, one of the "greenist" buildings in the world. It was wonderful to see these two buildings together.

We, I, had to start at the top, the third floor, because that is where the replica is of the oval office when Clinton occupied it. I couldn't get enough if it. Clinton narrates a description of the oval office and its furnishings and art. He also talks about coming there to work at night and on weekends. There is something magical about the space, if not always about the person who occupies it.

There are two exhibit spaces on the third floor. One is for traveling exhibits; the other is an exhibit of the Clinton presidential years from an informal perspective. When we were there the traveling exhibit was the history of the African American in America from the perspective of the presidents: who did what; what impact it made, etc. It was a fascinating way to reflect on the power of the presidency, as well as the function of courage, or lack thereof, in a president. Sometimes their wives had more courage than their husbands.

On the second floor is the timeline exhibit. This room was designed to reflect the architecture of the library at Trinity College in Dublin. A few years ago I spent an afternoon in the Trinity Library. It is the home of the Book of Kells which I wanted to see. I could see what the architect was trying to do with the Clinton Library, but it is a faint homage at best.

The timeline of the Clinton years is down the middle of the library. A series of alcoves on either side provide additional information on the issues that were central during that particular point in time. This room is worth a day by itself. I was delighted to find that the impeachment is included. What a contrast to the Nixon Library which makes no mention of Watergate.

Finally, on the second floor, is a replica of the Cabinet Room with an interactive system that allows you to explore the personnel and the issues that each cabinet member was wrestling with during the Clinton years. That room is also worth a day by itself.

I was fascinated to learn that cabinet members sit around the President in the order in which the cabinets were added to the government. The Secretary of State sits to the President's immediate right. Opposite is the Vice President.

After dinner we asked our trusty GPS to take us to Little Rock Central High School. We drove by that infamous site and talked about those nine children who braved the venom of the "cheerleaders" who gathered day after day to shout every racial epithet imaginable and spit at them as the children walked through the gauntlet to go to school. It was too late for the museum.

It was an exhilarating day in Little Rock.

Memories of Little Rock in 1957

The next morning Mary Ann wanted to go back to Central and go through the museum.

1957-58 was my senior year in high school. I remember watching the television news at night. I remember the formal debate topic that raised the question of the right to enforce a law when it endangered others. I remember Eisenhower appearing angry and disgusted at Orville Faubus as he announced on television that he was sending in the 101st Airborne. My parents were solid moderate Republicans who loved Ike. They were also solid integrationists. They were very proud of Ike. The museum includes the film clips from those days. Mike Wallace narrates the clips.

The museum includes newspaper reports, photographs, and memorabilia. It is not a large museum, but it is a moving one. What struck me is that it is there. I felt very proud of America. The pride was not in the despicable history or how far we have come. The pride was that we would build a museum to our tragic flaws and our halting steps towards making things right. This reflective capacity may be one of our unsung strengths.

It was a special Thanksgiving and I am glad that Arkansas was last.

Sicko – Another Lover's Quarrel From Michael Moore

Robert Frost's epitaph reads that he had a "Lover's quarrel with the world." Michael Moore has one with America. Lover's quarrels tend to be passionate because the caring is so deep. They also tend, like any quarrel, to use hyperbole and to build self-serving cases. Moore does all of this in Sicko, although to a lesser extent than his previous films.

I admit to wanting to quarrel with Moore. There is a lot to quarrel with in Sicko. The biggest quarrel I have is that he does not address the entire health care system. He acts as though we all buy individual policies from insurance carriers. Nothing could be further from the truth. Most Americans are insured through their employers. But Michael lets employers get off the hook. Perhaps in his search for villains he only wanted to select one – insurance companies. For example, he never points out that it is the employer who decides what benefits are to be covered and not covered. He blames the insurance companies for that. Wrong, Michael. Do you not know; or do you not care?

One example is blatant. He uses a clip of Dr. Janet Peeno testifying before Congress. She describes her pain at having to reject a man's desire for a heart transplant because it "wasn't covered." The way Moore presents it one would think that it was the decision of the insurance company. Wrong, Michael. The employer had chosen to purchase a plan that did not include a heart transplant as a benefit.

Damned, I wish Michael would get his facts straight because he shoots himself in the foot with this kind of inaccuracy and nonsense. And, if one knows a system, it makes it hard to take him seriously. And he should be taken seriously.

His comparisons with the single payer systems of Canada, France, Germany and the UK need to be taken seriously. The citizens of those countries do have better health outcomes than Americans enjoy. Of course they are not perfect systems, but they are better systems.

You do have to smile with Michael and enjoy the political theater of a trip to Cuba with rescue workers from 9-11 because the involuntary guests of our prison there get better health care than we are providing to our own people. The Cubans, of course, are more than willing to provide care to these folks – free of charge of course. Let us not forget that Cuba also offered to provide aid to our people in New Orleans after that disaster, and this was before the U.S. Government turned its back on our fellow citizens there.

This is the core of Michael's quarrel. He wants us to care more and, when it comes to health, he wants us to provide more care – for all of our neighbors. And it is a lover's quarrel because it is based on compassion and caring. What he accuses us of is becoming so entrenched in a market economy that we refuse to see what we are doing to ourselves.

So, while we can quarrel with Michael – we will always be able to do that – we have to understand that he is trying to shake us out of our lethargy so we can become better, and that's what good lovers do. They challenge us to want to become our best selves.

November

"Get here a little before noon
so you can pull your boat right into the slings."

The boat yard confirmed the time,
Sunday at noon,
At the height of the tide
Because the designer wanted a boat
That would be stiff in a blow
And drew her a deep keel.

It's the end of October and
The family is making plans
For Thanksgiving and Christmas.
Sadness and joy mix as dates and commitments
Come now on email, disembodied more
Than ever before-- increasing distance.

My grandmother's house was next door.
They lived on the second floor
With my aunt and uncle
And adopted cousin a floor below.
Plans were made then
In footsteps, kitchen smells, and
The constant kettle for tea or cocoa
Depending on your age.

I said I'd have the boat there
Precisely at noon,
When the tide was high.

Driving home from the yard,
Sails folded in bags,
Unused supplies sorted and packed,
Darkness has come too soon
And I wonder how many more
Summers I have to sail.
(Measuring time in summers has always
seemed natural in New England – the taking out
and putting away, the opening and closing.)

It is truly the end of the month,
And the darkness has closed this summer away.

The Knee and the Boat

The love affair began with a knee and a boat. It was the summer of nineteen seventy-seven. First came the knee. My thirteen-year-old daughter Becky, who became Rebecca some time during her twenties, had a knee that was constantly causing her trouble. Every time she bumped it she would develop what is erroneously called "water on the knee." A rheumatologist referred her to the head of orthopedics at Yale New-Haven hospital. This led to an operation on her knee that was and is too gruesome to discuss in detail, but it was sufficiently fascinating that her rheumatologist scrubbed in as an observer. Becky was amazingly subdued before and immediately after the procedure. She was tired of the pain associated with the knee and having to have it elevated with ice packs and all that went with it. No fun for a teenager.

The rehabilitation, though, was anything but subdued. Rehabilitation called for on-going physical therapy so she did not lose flexibility in the new lining growing within the knee. The bending and straightening exercises were painful, very painful. She had to exercise at home; she had to exercise with a physical therapist. It was one of those parental times when empathy, trusting the doctor's advice, and having to be the "bad guy," was stressful for the father although not as painful as the exercises were for the daughter. Pain was pain and she had no hesitation making that known.

Divorced at the time, my children would spend every August with me in addition to the every other weekend ritual. Becky's operation was in late May. The rehabilitation would stretch through the summer. Cruising on a sailboat for the month of August, the original plan for the summer of seventy-seven, was not going to take place. The new challenge was to find a place to vacation where Becky could continue the rehabilitation that she needed but would provide everyone, her older sister and her younger brother and her father and his live-in girlfriend, with enough activity, variety, and enjoyment that no one would become a self pitying menace for thirty days.

I thought that Becky should have a say in the vacation decision and that her needs should come first. Our first thought was Cape Cod. This was pre-internet, so it took a couple of telephone calls to find out that the physical therapy she would need was available on the Cape and so one weekend Becky and I left Southern Connecticut to go house hunting for an August rental on the Cape.

Sticker shock is a real phenomenon. It is a visceral reaction that combines surprise, disappointment, and a dash of anger. I'm not sure what my expectations were, but they had no relationship to Cape Cod summer rentals. I was thinking of paying for a month what it would cost for a week on the Cape. Still we looked. We then found that we were looking far too late to find a place that was big enough for us. More than one real estate broker shook a sad head and exhaled a woeful, "I don't know." This would be followed by a discussion of the inventory of rentals and how it was depleted to close to nothing and that the only thing that might be available would be a small cottage. We looked at some. The ones we looked at would have fit in my living room, and I had a small house. Five of us would not have survived.

Because it was a May weekend and the summer was close to getting underway, we also had our first experience sitting in Cape Cod traffic, both Saturday morning on the way out from Southern Connecticut and Sunday evening on the way back. Dismayed and depressed, Becky and I returned home to Connecticut.

And now the boat. It appeared in an advertisement in a boating magazine. My reaction was immediate and narcissistic. The advertisement was for the charter of a Stone Horse. I had fallen in love with the pictures and the description of this twenty-one foot sailboat when it first appeared in the design section of Cruising World. Built in Mattapoisette, Massachusetts, rigged as a cutter, the Stone Horse was and is a beautiful homage to traditional sailboat design combined with some later day engineering and ingenuity. And there were two available for charter in someplace with the unlikely name of Brooklin, Maine. My concern for involving Becky in the decision making surrendered to my intense need to charter that boat. It was far too small for us to live on board, but my imagination was plenty big enough to have us enjoying sailing in the islands of Maine with eagles above and seals emerging periodically from the water to look around and perhaps give a bark or two. Every sailor is a romantic, and most of us are impulsive to some degree. Both were at work.

A quick look at the map let me know it would be a long drive, and a little more searching let me know that Brooklin was a small town but there was a hospital, albeit small, about thirty minutes away in Blue Hill. A call to the hospital confirmed that they could handle the physical therapy. They had a physical therapist that came over from Bar Harbor twice a week. The surgeon was going to be in New Hampshire where the orthopedic department at Yale provided round robin physicians for a camp. It was going to mean a drive to New Hampshire for the monthly check up.

A call back to the number on the advertisement arranged for the charter of the boat for three of the four weeks in August – one week was already booked – and now all I needed was a place to house everyone. *Please let there be a place* was my prayer.

Dreading a repeat of the housing stock experience of the Cape, I convinced my then girlfriend, not yet wife, to go to Maine with me that weekend in search of a house. We left on a Friday night and drove as far as Portsmouth, New Hampshire, a four hour trek that was to feel like a commute to me as the years went by. The next morning we left very early and stayed on interstate ninety-five as far as Portland, Maine, and then we switched over to route one, that most American of roads that begins in Key West Florida and ends on the Maine-Canadian border. We had an appointment with a real estate broker at noon in Blue Hill so decided we would meander up route one and drive through the towns that I had read about for years in sailing magazines: Camden, Rockport, Belfast and the others. Taking this route would mean we could also make a quick stop in Freeport to visit LL Bean.

Route one finds its way through these towns, giving occasional glimpses of the water. As one proceeds East up the coast, the towns become farther apart and woods and fields replace strip malls and traffic lights. By the time we reached Blue Hill, we were smitten with the Maine Coast.

Blue Hill is as quaint and pretty as a town can be. But the broker responded with an, "Oh my," to my needs. My heart sank. She did her best, but she only had a few things she could show us; we looked. But nothing would work. However, she tossed out a life ring: "A lot of people don't list and things are rented by word of mouth. There's a colony over in Brooklin. There might be something there. Why don't you stop by the Post Office in Brooklin and ask the Postmistress. She might know of something."

So off we went to Brooklin. At least we could stop by the boatyard to see where the boat would be. It might already be in the water. I was already wondering if I might have to try to get out of the charter. Although we had made a commitment on the phone, it was only two days old.

The boat was not in the water. There were very few boats in the water and the ones that were, were working boats. No one was around. It was Saturday in May and summer had not started in Maine. The water though, the water off the dock, was crystal clear and we took a few minutes just to absorb the beauty of the harbor and the island that formed the harbor with its pines and granite shore. Later we would learn that the island's name was Chatto.

Back in the car we continued towards where the broker had told us the colony would be. We wanted to drive in and get some sense of the houses before we went to the post office. I was afraid that we might be repeating our Cape Cod experience and the colony would be filled with small cottages built upon one another. We found it and drove in.

These were not the small cottages of Cape Cod. To the right were beautiful homes with May gardens in bloom. To the left was a tennis court. It was too early in the season for players but one could clearly tell from the sign up sheet of the previous summer that this court was well used. And then the dirt road divided. One went to the right, another to the left, and the one we were on went straight. We went straight. There were more homes on either side. The road bent to the left and then to the right, opening up on the water. The "Yacht Club" at the end of the road was a simple wooden building with a porch. We stopped and got out.

"What do you think?"
"Love it."
"Think there will be any houses."

"I hope. I wonder what the prices will be like."

We returned to the car and started back up the hill.

"Let's take this road to the left."

We did and immediately stopped. The house on the left was shingled in weathered shakes with green shutters and trim. It looked like an advertisement for the Maine coast. We got out and walked around back. A field stretched down to a gravel beach. A porch ran across the entire back and side of the house. We looked in the windows. I could not imagine anything more perfect and I knew there was no way it could be for rent in August or that I could possibly afford it. But it was something dreams are made of.

We returned to the car and explored the other roads. There were wonderful places. Some were smaller, not on the water, and maybe one of those might be available and affordable.

We went to the Post Office. I wish I could remember the name of the postmistress. She was very helpful, but there was only one possibility she could think of. She gave us a name and a number to call. There was a pay phone outside the post office. I called. It was a Georgia number. The woman who answered was delightful. Yes, they did have a cottage in the colony; yes, it was available for rent in August. The price was exactly what I had budgeted. So where was it?

"You go past the tennis court, take your first right and it is the first house on your left."

It was done. It was ours for the month. We couldn't believe it. And then she told me about the yacht club, what it would cost to join, about the sailing lessons, who we had to call, and she was sure the kids would have a wonderful time. Her parents lived right across the street and would help us out with anything we needed. We made the necessary arrangements and exchanged information. When I hung up I couldn't help laughing and doing a little jig in the parking lot of the post office.

At the time I was the director of a leadership institute for the Planned Parenthood Federation of America. I worked with the management and boards of directors of that esteemed institution which did and does hold the loyalties of this former Catholic now Unitarian. I was to conduct a training session in Pennsylvania and, at some point during a break in the training, I mentioned to one of the board members that I was going to be spending my summer vacation in Brooklin. Silly as it was, I had developed this mildly amusing line of telling people I was going to vacation in Brooklin. They would immediately think of the borough of New York City named Brooklyn. Not known as a vacation destination, they would then look at me quizzically which was my invitation to add Maine to my sentence. This person did not look quizzical. Instead, she told me I had to talk to Nancy, one of the other board members.

I did. Nancy was excited to find out I was going to Brooklin and was sure that I would love it. She knew it well. Her brother had a summer place there and her half-brother, Joel, owned the largest business in Brooklin, the Brooklin Boat Yard.

Since her name was Stapleford and she didn't add anything else, it wouldn't be until August that the dots came together and the brother became Roger Angell of the *New Yorker*, and the half-brother was naval architect and boat builder Joel White. The other members of the family tree were not mentioned: her step-father E.B. White and her mother, Katherine White. To echo the real estate broker from Blue Hill, "Oh my."

As a former English teacher, I was of course familiar with Strunk and White's *Elements of Style*. As a father I had read *Charlotte's Web* and *Stuart Little* over and over again. And I had seen Katherine White's gardening books in my father's house. As a sailor I had been reading *Wooden Boat* as well as *Cruising World,* so knew of Joel White's designs. Some family.

Haven Colony is hard to describe. It has to be experienced. Ann River Siddons uses the Colony, with literary license of course, for two of her books: *Colony* and *Off Season*. Her descriptions of Colony life are much better than I could ever hope to achieve.

Ritual Colony would be an equally good name for "the Colony" as it was referred to by all of the families who went there summer after summer after summer, generation after generation after generation. The goal was to assure that nothing changed. There was a "Chowder Race," a "Deer Island Race," a square dance, and a BBQ every Thursday night where you brought your own food and cooked it down at the Yacht Club. There were races on the weekend and tea was served after the races.

We were renters who were different from owners. But we were all from "Away," that Maine appellation which discriminates between Maine people and summer people and newcomers. To say that the social stratification was clearly bounded is a modest use of the concept of social boundaries. Public school. Did anyone really go to public school? Thank the goddess that not everyone made it into the Ivies.

People were polite; people were welcoming. There were, though, very clear boundaries. They were formed by history, by class, and by concern for what family one originated from. He's a: _____ (fill in the blank). She's a: _____ (fill in the blank). What filled in the blanks communicated an amount of information that would crowd the floppy discs that were to come later. Of course _____ often married _____ and produced new generations of _____s who would go on to say that – you get it.

Alcoholism was prominently displayed with its accompanying destructive force of embarrassment for children and spouse and concern on the part of those who knew the person as a child or knew their spouse. The alcoholism was public. What I found notable was that it did not lead to ostracism. The "politeness" was maintained.

Given all of this, we inhaled the magic of the rituals, and in some instances were able to climb over the boundaries and begin the slow process of developing intimacy. And so we came back, and came back for several summers, to the same house and took the same bedrooms, and the kids would head for the Yacht Club as soon as the car stopped in front of the Klefane Cottage as it was known, the name attached from owners years before the current owners.

We acquired a dog from one of the "owners," and I bought a sailboat that could be trailed back and forth from Southern Connecticut. The boundaries, though, had largely been broken down by the children and, as could be expected, we started to talk about the "Colony" as though we had been going there for generations. We don't go there anymore, but at family reunions when someone mentions the "Colony" it is a family shorthand of wonderful Maine summers and it all began with a knee and a boat called Stone Horse.

Center Harbor

For Deborah and Rebecca
August 30, 1980

The moonglade landed on our beach
Our final night in Maine.
We stayed awake and watched its journey
Slowly moving down the Reach.

Moored, our boat nodded in the night
Trailing luminescent beads
As the tide began to ebb.
The loon laughed with delight.

Enough leaves had turned
To draw our comments out
About the varied colors
And that one tree that
Always started first.
We went inside and
Watched the fire burn.

Dressing for bed was simple ritual.
The wine had been good
But it was the windowed moon
That brought silence to the room.

Drawing down the shades
We closed the summer into memory.

Revolution and Evolution

My grandmother could not vote until she was thirty-seven. My mother was seven. My mother never missed voting as long as I can remember. As she got older she even started voting for Democrats. I was nineteen when the first Irish Catholic was elected President of the United States. My mother had told me it would never happen. Yes, she did vote for John Fitzgerald Kennedy.

More than half of the delegates at the convention this year were women. Hillary Clinton was almost our nominee. Nancy Pelosi is Speaker of the House. More than half of the graduates of law schools are women; half of the students in medical schools are women. More women graduate from college now than men. And still there is unequal pay, even when all variables like age, experience, and so on are held constant. And as much attention is given to the color of Michelle Obama's dress against the blue background of the stage as to what she said. What nonsense.

Gene often told me it would never happen and that I didn't understand, couldn't understand, how racist to the core America is. It was 1969. I do remember it was Gene who said it, which means we had to be in Georgia because that's where we worked together when we were a team training community organizers in the basements of churches. The voting rights act was only four years old and in some of the rural areas where we worked you would never have known that it had been passed. All of the "White – Colored" signs were still up and we used to ignore them as a matter of course. We were young, not yet thirty, and brash, and so I would always drink from the "Colored" fountain (I often had to go around to the back of the building to do so) and Gene would drink from the one marked "White." We were only serious some of the time.

Last night twenty of us sat in our living room and watched Barak Obama accept the nomination of the Democratic Party for the President of the United States. I wish I knew where Gene was today. I would have called him. Although I surely do love being proved right, I wouldn't have rubbed it in.

There were a lot of gray heads in our living room last night and one of the women and I swapped stories about 1973 and Roe v. Wade. She was working in a small Planned Parenthood clinic in the mid-west in 1973. I was working in the national office of Planned Parenthood in New York when the decision was announced. I later commented to my wife, Mary Ann, that one of our guests reminded me of the Planned Parenthood "little old ladies in tennis shoes" who used to drive women from Connecticut to New York so they could get their contraceptives prior to 1965 and the Supreme Court ruling regarding privacy in Griswold v. Connecticut. It was only eight years from Griswold to Roe. Most young people find it hard to believe Connecticut had a law against the use or sale of contraceptives.

Yesterday afternoon I dropped off some papers at our accountant's office. I invited him and his partner to join us last night. They have been together longer than Mary Ann and me. We're married. In 2007 in New York, they can't be. (As I edit this in 2012, they can be.)

Jennifer Taylor is a colleague, one of the most competent quantitative researchers I know. She works for Pfizer Health Solutions, a division within Pfizer that does public health work. We worked together as part of the core team that started Green Ribbon Health for seniors three years ago and then on the research committee afterwards. I remember asking Jennifer why she and her partner didn't move from Santa Monica to Tampa where Green Ribbon is based. She couldn't, she said, because Florida will not recognize her as co-mother to the daughter she and her partner are raising. Florida's loss. This will change. I don't know when, but it will change.

Of course I cried last night as well as cheered when Barak finished his speech. But it wasn't until later that the tears really flowed. Our guests had left, Mary Ann and I were cleaning up, but I stopped to watch the television when John Lewis was interviewed.

John Lewis is a year older than me. You couldn't work in the South during those years and not know about John. John had led SNCC, the Student Non-violent Coordinating Committee.

John had been badly beaten in Montgomery during the Freedom Rides and then again on the Selma to Montgomery March in 1965. And now he is in Congress. Last night he was asked dumb interview questions by a reporter who couldn't possibly understand the tectonic shift that had just taken place. John was polite and held it together. But then he started to talk about Mrs. Hamer and what last night would have meant to her. He became a bit teary. That did it for me. I didn't cry; I wept.

This morning, the day after Barak Obama has accepted the nomination, I realize how old I am and how fortunate. I am feeling old, not because of my chronological age, but because of what I want my grandchildren to understand. One of the gifts of the Seder ritual are the words about the need for every generation to take on the battles of its generation to free the human spirit. I am fortunate because I have been witness to, and have sometimes participated in, changes that some said could never happen.

I am absolutely confident that my grandchildren will witness more liberation during their lifetime. I no longer wonder if changes of this nature will take place. I am confident they will. My life experience has taught me to be confident. I do have a hope, though, for my grandchildren. I hope they learn that it's more meaningful, sometimes dangerous, and often scary, to be actively engaged in that process. Also, it can be a lot of fun. I hope for them the tears that come when the John Lewis of their generation sparks a memory of someone who moved them as deeply as Mrs. Hamer moved me.

Here we are in 2012 and Mary Ann and I are planning a long trip to see America, our own "Travels With Charley." Mary Ann has not been to Mississippi before. We will go there and we will stop by Ruleville, Mississippi. It seems like a very long time ago I first heard stories about Mrs. Hamer. It was before I had joined the Community Development Foundation, it was before I knew about Myles Horton and the Highlander Center, and even before I had been South of Washington, D.C. I sure didn't know much, but I knew this was a woman to be reckoned with.

The Wikipedia entry for Ruleville begins with a simple statement:

During the 20th Century African-American Civil Rights Movement, Fannie Lou Hamer, a farmworker, started a movement for poor people.

About the author:

Vaughn Keller has been a police officer, high school teacher, launch boy, university professor, boat captain, researcher, salesman, psychotherapist, bartender, and consultant. Along the way he has collected two masters degrees, a doctorate, three professional certificates, and more graduate credits than anyone should ever have.

Through it all he has written: short stories, professional articles, essays, poetry, and a novel, *Behind the Neon*. As a consultant, leader, teacher, and clinician, his day job(s) have focused on change: individual, organizational, societal. He has worked with and for large corporations and small community groups. He admits to being a professional change junkee.

He lives across the street from a pond in Plymouth, Massachusetts with his wife, Mary Ann Hergenrother, an elderly German Shepherd, Cara na Chroí, and a sprightly miniature poodle, Charley.

www.ingramcontent.com/pod-product-compliance
Lightning Source LLC
Chambersburg PA
CBHW071503040426
42444CB00008B/1474